LOOK INTO THE BIBLE

LOOK INTO THE BIBLE

Scripture Union
London   Sydney

CONTENTS

Acknowledgements

The photographs in this book are reproduced by kind permission of the following:

Gladys Aylward Trust 45
British Museum 30, 66 bottom, 122
Cephas Picture Library, 55, 58, 59, 83 top left, 88 centre, 108, 125 top right & bottom left
Church Missionary Society 47 centre
Mary Evans Picture Library 43 bottom left
Gordon Gray 17, 20 left, 21 top, 34, 37, 41, 43 top, 51, 67, 68, 72, 73, 79, 83 except top left, 88 left and bottom, 89 except top right, 93, ·102, 131
John Grayston 81
Greenleaf/Tear Fund 46, 125 centre right
International Films 47 left
Keston College 63, 130
Missionary Aviation Fellowship 113
Gill Rennie 66 top, 107, 111
John Rylands Library, University of Manchester 130 left
SCM Press 43 bottom centre
Shaftesbury Society 43 bottom right
Shell 14 bottom right, 65
Jamie Simson 20 centre, 27, 39
World Challenge Inc. 47 right
ZEFA 14 top, 21 bottom, 31, 89 top right 120, front cover

The quotation on page 135 from *The Last Battle* by C. S. Lewis is used by permission of the estate of C. S. Lewis and The Bodley Head.

British Library Cataloguing in Publication Data

Look into the Bible.
    1. Bible ——— Juvenile literature
   I. Scripture Union
     220   BS539

© Scripture Union 1988

First published 1988

ISBN 0 86201 487 5 UK
ISBN 0 85892 353 X AUSTRALIA

Published in UK by Scripture Union,
130 City Road, London EC1V 2NJ
Published in Australia by Anzea Publishers,
PO Box 115, Flemington Markets, NSW 2129

Phototypeset by
Input Typesetting Ltd, London SW19 8DR

Colour reproduction by J Film Process, Bangkok

Printed by New Interlitho, S.p.A, Milan

FOREWORD

For many children and young people the Bible is a closed book. Even when it is opened its message often appears obscure compared with the powerful slogans of today's media. The distant geography, the ancient culture, the complexities of history are all obstacles to understanding. Add to that the varieties of literature and the differing styles of the biblical authors telling their story against concepts of time and place quite different from our own and it is hardly surprising that many youngsters reject the Bible as boring, difficult or irrelevant. Yet if these barriers can be overcome, God's message can be understood and seen to be as applicable as it ever was.

Look into the Bible seeks to assist children in the upper junior/lower secondary age range to move from the immediate problems of understanding the words, the history and the culture of the Bible to hearing what God has to say about contemporary situations. In a way, it is a junior 'commentary' to the whole Bible.

Many people have been involved in creating this book. Using a variety of styles of writing, pictures, maps and diagrams, their one aim has been to draw the reader into the Bible and its world in order to show how God continues to meet people and communicate with them today.

Eric Gower, Consulting Editor

Consulting Editors
Eric Gower, Head of Teaching Resource Centre
Tony Lane, Lecturer, London Bible College

Writers
Jan King   The Acts of the Apostles
Mike Law   Genesis to Deuteronomy
Philip Neal   Isaiah to Malachi
Brian Reed   Acts to Revelation
Helen Robinson   Kings to Nehemiah
Chris Tarrant   Joshua to Kings
Geoff Treasure   The Gospels

Design
Tony Cantale Graphics

Illustrations
David Gifford
Richard Deverell
Anna Carpenter

Abbreviations

Books of the Bible

The following abbreviations are used for names of Bible books.

Old Testament

Gen	Genesis
Exod	Exodus
Lev	Leviticus
Num	Numbers
Deut	Deuteronomy
Josh	Joshua
Judg	Judges
Ruth	Ruth
Sam	Samuel
Kings	Kings
Chron	Chronicles
Ezra	Ezra
Neh	Nehemiah
Esther	Esther
Job	Job
Ps	Psalms
Prov	Proverbs
Eccl	Ecclesiastes
Song of Songs	Song of Songs
Isa	Isaiah
Jer	Jeremiah
Lam	Lamentations
Ezek	Ezekiel
Dan	Daniel
Hos	Hosea
Joel	Joel
Amos	Amos
Obad	Obadiah
Jon	Jonah
Mic	Micah
Nah	Nahum
Hab	Habakkuk
Zeph	Zephaniah
Hag	Haggai
Zech	Zechariah
Mal	Malachi

New Testament

Matt	Matthew
Mark	Mark
Luke	Luke
John	John
Acts	The Acts of the Apostles
Rom	Romans
Cor	Corinthians
Gal	Galatians
Eph	Ephesians
Phil	Philippians
Col	Colossians
Thess	Thessalonians
Tim	Timothy
Titus	Titus
Philm	Philemon
Heb	Hebrews
Jas	James
Pet	Peter
John	John
Jude	Jude
Rev	Revelation

Bible references

References to verses in the Bible are written like this:
Gen 8:22, which means Genesis chapter 8, verse 22.
Where several verses are included the reference is
written as Acts 4:1–22, which means Acts chapter 4
verses 1 to 22.

References are quoted from the Good News Bible.

THE WAY IN

Unpacking the Bible
The Bible is not like an ordinary book. It is a large collection of sixty-six separate books inside one cover. When we unpack them we find that the books are in two main sections:

The Old Testament – 39 books

The New Testament – 27 books

THE OLD TESTAMENT
Books about Jewish history and religion.
These can be arranged in four groups of books

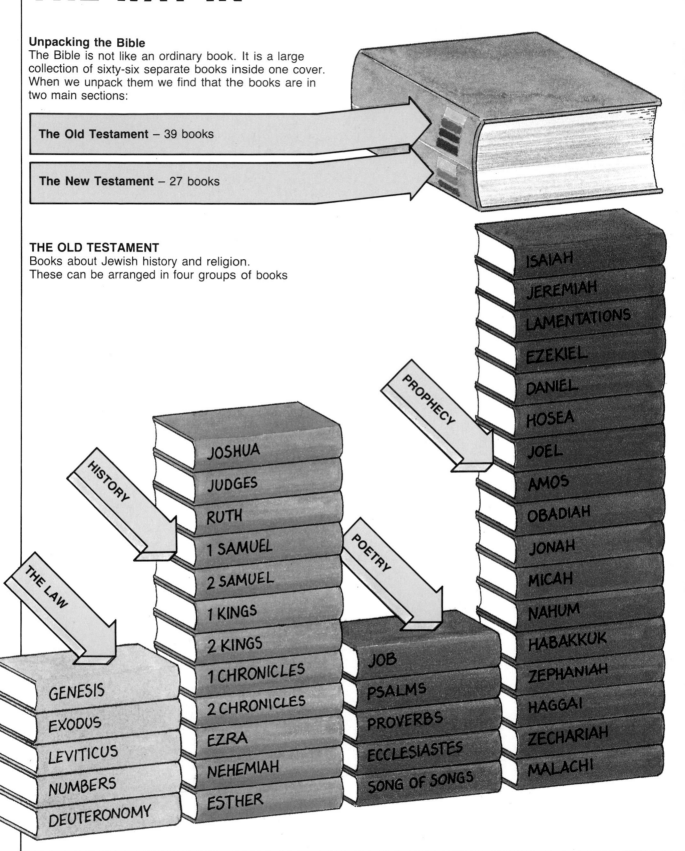

PROPHECY

ISAIAH
JEREMIAH
LAMENTATIONS
EZEKIEL
DANIEL
HOSEA
JOEL
AMOS
OBADIAH
JONAH
MICAH
NAHUM
HABAKKUK
ZEPHANIAH
HAGGAI
ZECHARIAH
MALACHI

HISTORY

JOSHUA
JUDGES
RUTH
1 SAMUEL
2 SAMUEL
1 KINGS
2 KINGS
1 CHRONICLES
2 CHRONICLES
EZRA
NEHEMIAH
ESTHER

POETRY

JOB
PSALMS
PROVERBS
ECCLESIASTES
SONG OF SONGS

THE LAW

GENESIS
EXODUS
LEVITICUS
NUMBERS
DEUTERONOMY

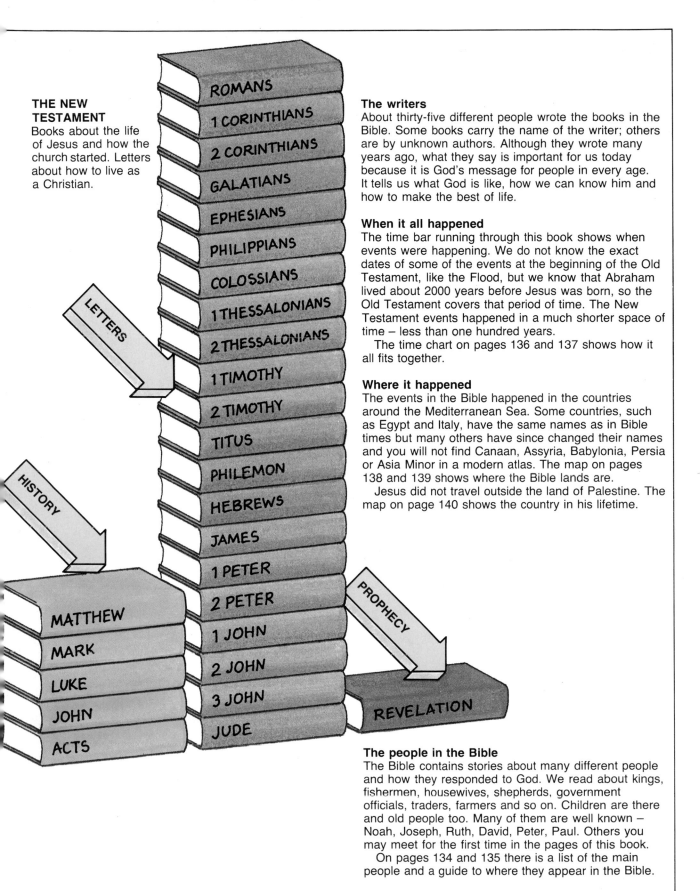

THE NEW TESTAMENT
Books about the life of Jesus and how the church started. Letters about how to live as a Christian.

LETTERS

HISTORY

PROPHECY

ROMANS
1 CORINTHIANS
2 CORINTHIANS
GALATIANS
EPHESIANS
PHILIPPIANS
COLOSSIANS
1 THESSALONIANS
2 THESSALONIANS
1 TIMOTHY
2 TIMOTHY
TITUS
PHILEMON
HEBREWS
JAMES
1 PETER
2 PETER
1 JOHN
2 JOHN
3 JOHN
JUDE

MATTHEW
MARK
LUKE
JOHN
ACTS

REVELATION

The writers
About thirty-five different people wrote the books in the Bible. Some books carry the name of the writer; others are by unknown authors. Although they wrote many years ago, what they say is important for us today because it is God's message for people in every age. It tells us what God is like, how we can know him and how to make the best of life.

When it all happened
The time bar running through this book shows when events were happening. We do not know the exact dates of some of the events at the beginning of the Old Testament, like the Flood, but we know that Abraham lived about 2000 years before Jesus was born, so the Old Testament covers that period of time. The New Testament events happened in a much shorter space of time – less than one hundred years.

The time chart on pages 136 and 137 shows how it all fits together.

Where it happened
The events in the Bible happened in the countries around the Mediterranean Sea. Some countries, such as Egypt and Italy, have the same names as in Bible times but many others have since changed their names and you will not find Canaan, Assyria, Babylonia, Persia or Asia Minor in a modern atlas. The map on pages 138 and 139 shows where the Bible lands are.

Jesus did not travel outside the land of Palestine. The map on page 140 shows the country in his lifetime.

The people in the Bible
The Bible contains stories about many different people and how they responded to God. We read about kings, fishermen, housewives, shepherds, government officials, traders, farmers and so on. Children are there and old people too. Many of them are well known – Noah, Joseph, Ruth, David, Peter, Paul. Others you may meet for the first time in the pages of this book.

On pages 134 and 135 there is a list of the main people and a guide to where they appear in the Bible.

THE BEGINNING OF A NATION
GENESIS, EXODUS, LEVITICUS, NUMBERS, DEUTERONOMY

The first five books of the Old Testament are sometimes called the Pentateuch. Pentateuch simply means 'five books' (or literally 'five scrolls'). Other names for them include 'The Books of Moses', 'The Law of Moses', 'The Book of the Law'. Jesus referred to it in his teaching, eg Luke 24:27. These five books are a very important part of all the Old Testament teaching.

GENESIS
A book of beginnings: The beginning of the universe. The beginning of life. A new beginning after the flood. The beginning of God's chosen people – Abraham, Isaac, Jacob and Joseph.

DEUTERONOMY
Another book of laws, and of looking back at what God has done for the people. It also looks forward to the blessing God will give the people if they remain true to him.

EXODUS
A book of escapes: Escape for baby Moses. Escape for the Israelites from Egypt. Escape through the Red Sea. Escape from the old way of life as God gives new laws.

NUMBERS
Not a maths book but a book of problems! Problems with counting the Israelites, problems with the food, problems with Miriam and Aaron, problems with conquering Canaan, problems with rebellion by the people, problems with the poisonous snakes, problems with the report of the spies.

LEVITICUS
A book of laws: Laws about offerings and sacrifices, laws about good food and illnesses, laws about dry rot and damp, laws about sex and marriage, laws about slaves and Sabbaths, laws about priests and worship, laws about feasts and festivals.

The Writer
These books themselves tell us that Moses wrote certain parts of them, see Exodus 24:4 and Numbers 33:2. It is likely that the five books we have in our Bible now are largely the work of Moses which have been edited at some later date.

GENESIS
CREATION, FLOOD AND THE PATRIARCHS

2000 BC	1900	1800
/ABRAHAM	/ISAAC	/JACOB & ESAU /JOSEPH

CREATION: MADE AND SPOILED

The first chapter of Genesis describes how God created the earth out of nothing. He made it in this order:

1. light and darkness

2. the sky

3. earth with plants and trees, the sea

4. sun, moon and stars

5. birds and fish

6. animals and man

When he had finished he saw that everything he had made was perfect. (Genesis 1:31)

God gave the first man, Adam, and the first woman, Eve, care of the animals and of the Garden of Eden. They were free to eat the fruit of any of the trees of the garden, except the tree that gave knowledge of what is good and what is evil.

Then . . .
- the serpent tempted
- Eve listened
- Eve ate the fruit
- Eve gave to Adam
- and nothing was the same again

Genesis tells us that God created the world by his command. Some scientists believe in the theory that the world evolved from nothing. Although scientists can observe and experiment and work out how things happen even they are not agreed on exactly how the world began.

Scientific theories change. It is probable that theories about the origins of the universe and of human life will also change. The Bible is not a science text book and we do not expect scientific information from it about how God created the world.

The beauty and order of creation seen in a tiny flower, a snowflake or a high mountain peak are evidence that it is the work of a great designer: God. These things could not have happened by chance.

The results of Adam and Eve's disobedience are certainly with us today. The world is in a mess which thousands of years of civilisation haven't been able to sort out.

Why is the world like this? Because the people who make up this world – and that means each of us – do not live in the way God wants. Look at the newspaper headlines. Many of the world's problems are caused by the same things we see in our own lives – greed, anger, jealousy. Adam and Eve's disobedience was the start of the rebellion against God which is still in our world today.

FAMINE
THOUSANDS IN DES

AMBUSHED BY

WAR IN TH

'I HATE YOU!'

13

THE FLOOD

Some people would like to see the judgement of God in every disaster. Although such things are the result of living in a spoilt world, and frequently the result of 'human error', Jesus made it clear that they are not judgements of an angry God on specially wicked people. See Luke 13:4.

PUNISHMENT

In the days of Noah God did send a disaster as a punishment for man's wickedness. The rebellion against God, started in the Garden of Eden, had spread so much that God could find only one good man, Noah, in the whole earth. God was sad that men had brought judgement on themselves by their disobedience. He decided to start again with Noah and his family. By obeying God's instructions to build the ark, Noah and his family were saved, along with some of every species of animal.

PROMISE

God's promise (Genesis 9:8–17) was that he would never again destroy all living creatures by flood. There have been many natural disasters since then but they have affected limited areas for limited times and are part of living in a spoilt world. The destruction of all mankind except for Noah and his family did not restore the world to its original perfect condition.

Noah's Ark was 150 metres long, 25 metres wide and 15 metres high. This oil tanker is 169 metres long, 26 metres wide and 48 metres high.

A NEW START!

Peter, writing thousands of years later (1 Peter 3:20–21), tells us that the story of Noah's ark has a special meaning for us. Just as Noah and his family were saved from death and given a new start, so we are offered God's forgiveness and a new start because of Jesus' death for us.

SPOTLIGHT ON
ABRAHAM

Educated Abraham came from the city of Ur. In the ruins of Ur many clay tablets have been found with records of sales between merchants and traders. Abraham was a wealthy man who could probably read and write. If he could not, he would have employed a scribe to keep records for him.

Religious People worshipped the moon god in Ur. We do not know how Abraham came to know the true God but we do know that when God spoke to him Abraham responded (Genesis 12:1–3).

Adventurous Abraham was seventy-five years old when God told him to pack up and leave home.

He obeyed without knowing where God would lead him. In fact, he spent the rest of his life living in a tent and moving from place to place.

Trusting Abraham trusted God to lead him to the country which he had promised (Genesis 12:1).

- Abraham trusted God when he promised that his descendants would be more than the stars in the sky (Genesis 15:5,6).
- Abraham trusted God when God asked him to offer his son, Isaac, as a sacrifice (Genesis 22).
- God chose Abraham to be the founder of the Jewish nation and all God's promises came true.

Abraham's travels from Ur to Canaan and Egypt

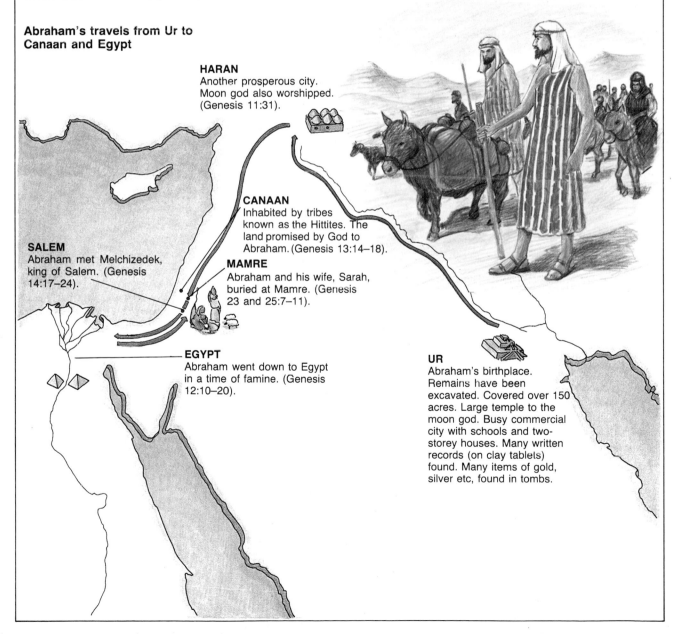

HARAN
Another prosperous city. Moon god also worshipped. (Genesis 11:31).

CANAAN
Inhabited by tribes known as the Hittites. The land promised by God to Abraham.(Genesis 13:14–18).

SALEM
Abraham met Melchizedek, king of Salem. (Genesis 14:17–24).

MAMRE
Abraham and his wife, Sarah, buried at Mamre. (Genesis 23 and 25:7–11).

EGYPT
Abraham went down to Egypt in a time of famine. (Genesis 12:10–20).

UR
Abraham's birthplace. Remains have been excavated. Covered over 150 acres. Large temple to the moon god. Busy commercial city with schools and two-storey houses. Many written records (on clay tablets) found. Many items of gold, silver etc, found in tombs.

FOLLOWING A FAMILY

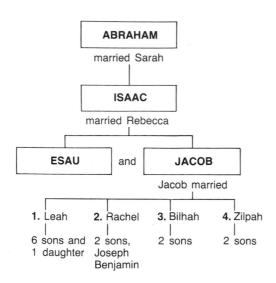

```
        ┌─────────────────┐
        │    ABRAHAM      │
        └─────────────────┘
          married Sarah
        ┌─────────────────┐
        │     ISAAC       │
        └─────────────────┘
         married Rebecca
   ┌──────────────┐     ┌──────────────┐
   │    ESAU      │ and │    JACOB     │
   └──────────────┘     └──────────────┘
                        Jacob married
  1. Leah      2. Rachel     3. Bilhah    4. Zilpah
  6 sons and   2 sons,       2 sons       2 sons
  1 daughter   Joseph
               Benjamin
```

ABRAHAM'S FAMILY TREE

The rest of the book of Genesis tells the story of Abraham's descendants. God promised Abraham that he would be the founder of a great nation. Abraham and his wife Sarah had one son, Isaac, who was born when they were old (Gen 21:1–7).

Isaac When Isaac was a boy, God tested Abraham's obedience by telling him to sacrifice Isaac. Abraham must have wondered how God could keep his promise of many descendants if Isaac were killed. But Abraham trusted God. Genesis 22:1–19 tells the whole story.

When it came time for Isaac to marry, Abraham did not want him to marry a Canaanite woman because they did not worship God. Abraham sent one of his servants to choose a wife from his home country. Genesis 24 tells the story of the servant's successful search for a wife and his return with Rebecca.

Esau and Jacob Rebecca and Isaac had twin sons, Esau and Jacob. Esau, born just before Jacob, had the privileges given to the eldest son. These included inheriting twice as much as his brother and becoming leader of the family when his father died. Jacob took advantage of his brother's hunger one day to persuade him to sell these birth rights for a pot of soup (Gen 25:27–30). Later he dressed up and pretended to be Esau to trick his father into giving him the blessing meant for Esau (Gen 27). Esau was so angry he planned to kill Jacob. Jacob ran away to stay with his uncle Laban for a while.

On the way God gave Jacob a special promise of protection (Gen 28:10–22).

Jacob worked for Laban for 14 years and married his daughters, Leah and Rachel.

Joseph Jacob had a large family of twelve sons and one daughter but his favourite son was Joseph. Jacob gave him a special coat which made his brothers very jealous. They disliked Joseph even more when he started to tell about the special dreams he had.

Eventually, the brothers took their chance to get rid of Joseph by selling him to slave traders going to Egypt.

The amazing story of how Joseph rose from being a slave to become prime minister of Egypt is told in Genesis 39–41.

Abraham, Isaac, Jacob and their families lived in tents. They moved site only when their sheep and goats needed new pasture. The women wove tent coverings from goats' hair and clothing from sheep's wool.

JOSEPH
THE MAN AT THE TOP

The Pharaohs

Tutankhamun is probably the best known of all the kings of Egypt. He died about 1350 BC, around ten years before Moses was born.

Pharaoh was not the name of an Egyptian king, but the title used by all the kings. We do not know the name of the pharaoh of Joseph's time.

By the time of Joseph, Egypt had a long history of civilisation – the pyramids had been built around 1,000 years earlier. Joseph's plans for collecting, storing and distributing grain were made possible probably by using the well developed 'civil service'.

THE MAN THEY COULDN'T KEEP DOWN

The Bible tells how Joseph always rose to the top whatever the situation. He arrived in Egypt as a slave but soon became chief servant in charge of Potiphar's house. Put in prison, he was given special responsibility for looking after the other prisoners and for the smooth running of the prison.

Finally his interpretation of the king's dream and his plan to deal with the famine brought Joseph to become Number Two in Egypt – the king's Prime Minister. The ring with the royal seal, the robe, the gold chain, the chariot and the guard of honour (Gen 41:42–43) were all marks of his appointment.

Joseph believed that God had planned all that happened to him. Things which seemed to be bad for Joseph were used for the good of a large number of people (Gen 50:20).

TODAY

The lives of Abraham and his descendants 4,000 years ago were very different from our lives today. The real importance of these stories in Genesis is that they show that God is interested in the lives of his people. They were ordinary people like us who made mistakes and disobeyed God. He continued to love and care for them as he will for us today.

Today we have a situation where in many countries there are huge storehouses full of grain, butter, wine and so on. We have more food than we know what to do with. In many other parts of the world thousands are dying of starvation and disease. National and international fund raising events have raised money for the hungry and have shown our ability to help. But there is still a long way to go before everyone in the world has a fair share.

EXODUS
SLAVES IN EGYPT

1400 BC	1350	1300
	/MOSES	THE EXODUS/

SLAVES IN EGYPT

The book of Exodus continues the story of Joseph's descendants. Joseph's eleven brothers and their families, seventy people in all, settled in Egypt. After Joseph and his brothers died, their descendants went on living there and their numbers grew. After several hundred years, there were so many of them that the Pharaoh was afraid that these foreigners, called Israelites, might turn against him. He decided to use them as slaves to build new cities.

It was hard and dirty work, making mud bricks, and the Egyptian slave drivers beat the Israelites if they did not work hard enough.

MOSES

Moses was the child of Israelite slaves but was brought up by the daughter of Pharaoh. The story of how she found him in a basket on the river is found in Exodus 2.

Moses was probably given a good Egyptian education. He would have learned to read and write hieroglyphic script. Probably he learnt archery and may have been an overseer on some of the Pharaoh's building work.

When he was forty, Moses killed an Egyptian in a fight (Exodus 2:11–16). He ran away to the desert and spent the next forty years looking after sheep. Here he learnt how to find water and how to survive in a desert.

God spoke to Moses one day from a burning bush in the desert and told him he wanted him to lead the Israelites out of Egypt (Exodus 3).

What Moses learned in Egypt and in the desert were good preparation for leading the Israelites from Egypt to the land of Canaan. But much was to happen before they left Egypt.

HOW TO MAKE A BRICK
1. Dig out mud.
2. Mix with water, treading it to get the right consistency.
3. Add chopped straw for strength. (About 20kg straw per cubic metre of bricks.)
4. Press into wooden frames.
5. Stamp the monarch's name on the side of each brick.
6. Leave to dry in the hot sun for 2 or 3 days.

PHARAOH VERSUS GOD

God sent Moses to ask Pharaoh to allow the Israelites to leave Egypt. Pharaoh refused and kept on refusing in spite of the disasters God sent (Exodus 7–11).

1. All water turned to blood.

2. Egypt full of frogs.

3. Gnats everywhere.

4. Flies covered everything.

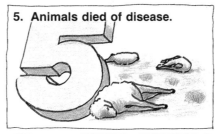

5. Animals died of disease.

6. People and animals covered with boils.

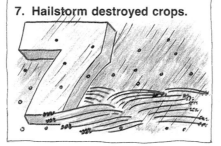

7. Hailstorm destroyed crops.

After the ninth disaster, Moses called the Israelites together and gave them these instructions to secure their safety (Exodus 12:1–14).

1. Choose a perfect, healthy lamb or goat.
2. Kill it and paint some of its blood on your doorposts.
3. Roast the meat and eat all of it with herbs and bread without yeast (unleavened bread).
4. Be ready with all your belongings to leave Egypt.

8. Locusts ate all plants.

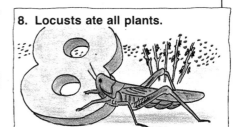

9. Darkness for three days.

10. Death of all first-born, including animals.

This was the first Passover festival. The name comes from the angel of death passing over the homes of the Israelites when he saw the blood on their doorpost. The Passover was celebrated every year to remind the people of their escape from Egypt. It is still celebrated by Jews today.

It was at the time of the Passover that Jesus had his last supper with his disciples and gave new meaning to the celebration. Like the Passover lamb, which died so that the eldest son could be saved, Jesus died to save us (see page 25).

EXODUS
JOURNEY TO FREEDOM

The Israelites travelled from Egypt through the desert to the land of Canaan. This was also known as 'The Promised Land' because God had promised it to Abraham and his descendants. It would be a distance of about 300 miles by a direct route but the Israelites spent over forty years in the desert. These pages show some of the things which happened on the way.

NO BRIDGE! NO BOATS!
Soon after they left Egypt, the people faced their first big test. The Egyptian army was behind them, the sea in front. There was no way across (Exod 14).

The Bible tells us that God used a strong east wind to divide the water. This was a great miracle and an important event to which people often looked back.

FIGHT FOR WATER
The Amalekites were nomad tribes who wandered the desert. They attacked the Israelites who were competing with them for the limited water and grazing which was available. Eventually Joshua went out to fight a decisive battle against them. As Joshua and the army fought, Moses prayed to God. See Exodus 17:8–16.

THE TEN COMMANDMENTS
God gave Moses laws for the people at Mount Sinai.

Mediterranean Sea

GOSHEN

EGYPT

Kadesh-barnea

The Bedouin still use animal skins as containers for liquid as the Israelites would have done.

An oasis in the Sinai Desert.

The Sinai Range.

Marah

Sinai Desert

Elim

Rephidim

Mount Sinai

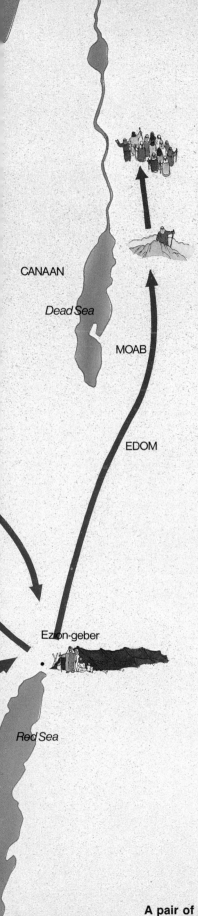

CANAAN

Dead Sea

MOAB

EDOM

Ezion-geber

Red Sea

A pair of quail.

The Israelites spent forty years wandering in the Sinai Desert.

NO ENTRY!

At the border of Canaan Moses sent twelve spies to see what the country was like. They all saw that it was a good fertile land. Ten of the twelve could see only the problems of invading Canaan. However, two of them believed in God's power to help them. Because the people refused to obey God and go into Canaan they had to spend forty years wandering in the desert until a whole generation had died. (Numbers 13 and 14).

People often call something a 'whatsitsname' or a 'thingumajig'. When the people saw the food which God had provided they said 'what is it?' – in their language 'man hu' and that is how manna got its name (Exod 16:15,31).

SURVIVAL

If you are going to survive long in the desert then two things are absolutely essential – water and food. The Israelites had been used to a settled, civilised life in Egypt where their diet would have included meat and fish, cucumbers, water melons, leeks, onions and garlic. They weren't prepared for desert life and when things got tough they began to moan.

At Marah the water was bitter (Exod 15:23). At Rephidim they couldn't find water (Exod 17:1) and in each case God used Moses to work a miracle and provide water. In some places, like Elim (Exod 15:27) water was plentiful.

God told Moses that food would drop out of the sky. It must have seemed unlikely but it happened with the quails and the manna. Quails migrate across the Sinai desert and, if exhausted by their journey, could have been easily caught by the people. God's provision of food for such a large number of people for a period of forty years was still a miracle.

A pair of quail.

'I AM THE LORD YOUR GOD WHO BROUGHT YOU OUT OF EGYPT'

God had chosen Israel to be his special people. He expected them to share his character and he gave them detailed rules for living.

These rules included:

- how to get along with each other
- how to settle disputes
- what is safe to eat
- how to worship God

The detailed rules are based on the Ten Commandments (Exod 20:1–17). These are in two sections.

1. Our relationship with God

1st commandment: Worship no other God
2nd commandment: Do not worship any images
3rd commandment: Do not use God's name for evil purposes
4th commandment: Keep God's day holy

2. Our relationship with others

5th commandment: Respect your parents
6th commandment: Do not commit murder
7th commandment: Do not commit adultery
8th commandment: Do not steal
9th commandment: Do not accuse anyone falsely
10th commandment: Do not desire other people's possessions

Jesus summed them up like this:
'Love the Lord your God with all your heart and with all your soul and with all your mind and strength and love your neighbour as you love yourself' (Mark 12:30,31).

HEALTH RULES

Life in the desert was completely different from life in Egypt. The people needed to learn some very practical rules about

- what food to eat. Leviticus chapter 11 lists birds and animals not to be eaten, including pigs and rabbits.
- how to deal with disease (Lev 13). People with infectious diseases were to be kept separate from the others to stop disease spreading.

These rules were God's way of keeping his people healthy.

GETTING ON TOGETHER

Problems were bound to occur with over 600,000 people living together (Num 1:46). It was essential that there were clear rules to deal with these situations. Feuds could have developed which would have seriously weakened the people. Among the subjects covered by the laws are:

- slaves (Exod. 21:1–11)
- violence (Exod 21:12–26)
- animals (Exod 21:28–36)
- theft (Exod 22:1–15)
- lies (Exod 23:1–3)
- marriage (Lev 18)

DO WE NEED LAWS?

If God had not given rules to his people in the desert they would not have survived. Rules are part of God's survival kit for us and are every bit as essential as food and water.

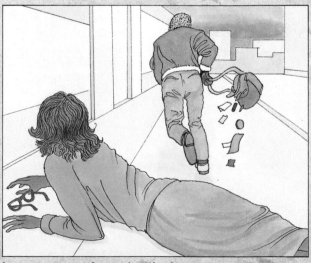

In many countries today the laws about our behaviour towards others reflect the Ten Commandments.

TABERNACLE

God gave Moses detailed instructions for the building of a special Tent (tabernacle is an old word for tent). This was to be used for the worship of God (Exod 25 onwards). It was not a tent in the sense that we usually think of it. Much of it was not roofed over but consisted of an open area enclosed by walls made of material supported on frames.

While in Egypt the people would have learnt many skills in building and craft work. This included embroidery, leather work and working with gold, silver and precious stones. They had materials which were given to them by the Egyptians (Exod 12:35–36).

Inside the Tent were:
1. The Covenant Box (also known as the Ark of the Covenant): A box of wood plated with gold. On the lid were two golden winged creatures (cherubim) (Exodus 25:10–22). Inside were kept the ten commandments, a pot of manna and Aaron's rod (Num 17:10).
2. A table of wood: covered with gold, for the bread which was offered to God.
3. The lampstand: made of gold, holding seven lamps (Exodus 25:23–40).

4. The altar: made of wood covered with bronze and used for sacrifices (Exodus 27:1–8).
5. A bronze basin: for the priests to wash in before performing any religious ceremony (Exodus 30:17–21).

PRIESTS AND LEVITES
The priests had to do the work of making sacrifices and offerings. Aaron, Moses' brother, was the first High Priest and only descendants of Aaron could become priests.

The High Priest was the only person allowed to go into the Most Holy Place in the Tent where he met with God.

The priests also taught the people the laws which God had given to Moses.

The whole tribe of Levi was set aside to help the priests in their work. They were known as Levites and one of their jobs was to carry the tent when the people moved camp.

When we worship God today we no longer need a tabernacle. Nor do we need a priest to speak to God for us. We can pray to God direct ourselves and know that he hears us.

LEVITICUS
LAWS AND WORSHIP

1300 BC	1250	1200

THE EXODUS

FESTIVALS

The worship of God was both serious and joyful. God gave the people a number of feasts which celebrated different events through the year. During these festivals there would be special sacrifices and offerings. On some, like the Day of Atonement, there would be fasting – no one would be allowed to eat anything. On others, like the Passover, there would be special meals.

New Moon
(Num 28:11)
The beginning of each month
A time for special offerings to God.

Passover & Unleavened Bread
(Lev 23:5, Num 28:16)
14–21 Nisan (April)
To celebrate the escape from Egypt and God passing over the Israelite children (see page 19)

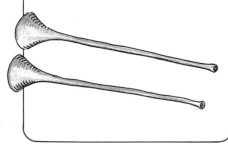

Day of Atonement
(Lev 23:26, Num 29:7)
10 Tishri (October)
To make special offerings for the sin of the people. The one day in the year when the High Priest goes into the Most Holy Place.

The Sabbath Year
(Lev 25:2, Deut 15:1)
Every 7th year
Debts were cancelled. The land was left uncultivated for the year.

Feast of Weeks or Harvest
(Later called Pentecost)
(Lev 23:15, Num 28:26)
6 Sivan (June)
To offer to God the first crop at the beginning of the harvest

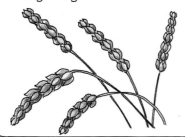

Feast of Shelters or Tabernacles
(Lev 23:33)
15–21 Tishri (October)
To remind the people of their time in the wilderness they built shelters of branches to live in for the week.

The Jubilee Year
(Lev 25:8)
Every 50th year
All land that had been sold was returned to its original owner. All Israelite slaves were set free.

The Sabbath
(Exod 20:8, Deut 5:12)
Every week on the 7th day of the week
To remind the people of God's timetable for creation. A day of rest and worship. No work at all was permitted.

Feast of Trumpets
(Lev 23:23, Num 29:1)
1–2 Tishri (October)
To celebrate the New Year

COVENANTS

The sacrifices, the tabernacle, the feasts and all the rules God gave the people were part of a special agreement between God and his people. In its simplest form the people agreed to obey the laws which God had given them and God promised to care for and protect his people. The Bible calls this agreement a 'covenant'. Today the word 'covenant' is only used in legal documents but it still means the same thing, a binding agreement between two parties.

SCAPEGOAT

Adam and Eve's disobedience resulted in their separation from God. Sin always separates between God and man. If the relationship is to be restored, sin must be dealt with. The sacrifices were God's way of dealing with sin.

One of the sacrifices offered by the High Priest used two goats. On the Day of Atonement one goat was killed and its blood sprinkled on the Covenant Box in the Most Holy Place. The High Priest then put his hands on the other goat and confessed the sins of the people. These were transferred to the goat who was then sent out into the desert to carry away the sins of the people. The word 'scapegoat' is used to mean someone who has to take the blame for something. Like many of the sacrifices, the scapegoat is a picture of Jesus and his work of 'carrying away' our sins (Lev 16).

SACRIFICES

Worship for the people of Israel must have been quite a messy affair. Although there were offerings of crops, flour and wine most sacrifices involved the death of animals and the pouring out or daubing of blood. To us it all seems rather gruesome. Why should God tell his people to worship in this way?

All the most important sacrifices were connected with sin. Sin is disobeying God. The basic idea of sacrifice was that the sin of the people was placed on the animal which then died as a substitute for the people. The blood represents the life of the animal. So pouring out the blood of the animal represents the offering of an innocent life to God as a substitute for the sinful life which needed to be punished.

Over a thousand years passed before Jesus, the Son of God, came to earth. Jesus was the only man who never disobeyed God.

Jesus died on the cross for our sin, just as the animals were sacrificed as a substitute for those who had sinned. His was the last great sacrifice for our sin. No more animal sacrifices were necessary.

NUMBERS AND DEUTERONOMY
ADVENTURES IN THE DESERT

1300 BC	1250	1200

/JOSHUA

OPERATION SPY (Numbers 13,14)
When the Israelites reached the borders of Canaan, Moses chose twelve men, one from each tribe, and sent them as spies to explore the land of Canaan. They were to report on the state of the land for cultivation, the size and construction of the cities, and the people who lived there. They were also to bring back a sample of the produce of the land.

The spies found a rich and fertile land with strong, fortified cities but they differed in their recommendations. Only two spies, Joshua and Caleb, had enough faith to believe that God would help them overcome the difficulties and give them the land he had promised. The other ten spies persuaded the people that the land was not worth conquering and that they would not stand a chance against the fierce inhabitants anyway.

The people's lack of trust in God resulted in forty years wandering in the desert. None of that generation, except Caleb and Joshua, were to enter the Promised Land.

NO WAY THROUGH (Numbers 20,21)
On their journey to Canaan the Israelites had to cross land belonging to other nations. Moses asked the king of Edom for permission to use The King's Highway, a good road leading north through his kingdom. He refused and backed up his refusal by appearing with a large army. The Israelites gave up and went round Edom.

Later, the Israelites asked the Amorite king, Sihon, for permission to pass through his territory. He replied by attacking them. In the battle that followed the Amorites came off worse and lost some of their territory to Israel. News of this defeat reached the king of Moab who decided to adopt a different tactic. He sent for a prophet, Balaam, to curse the Israelites. Balaam was reluctant at first. He finally agreed but told the king that he could only say what God wanted him to say. His prophecies turned out to be blessings on Israel, to the annoyance of the king of Moab (Numbers 22–24).

NOTHING BUT COMPLAINTS
(Numbers 21:4–9)

'We're fed up with this hard life in the desert!'

Although time and time again the people saw God provide what they needed, life in the desert was not easy. The people regularly complained and constantly needed to be challenged and disciplined by God. Once they were plagued with poisonous snakes as a result of their complaints. But God never deserted his people and even in punishing them was ready to show mercy. Moses was told to make a metal snake and to place it on a pole in the camp. If anyone was bitten by a snake they had only to

look at the metal snake to be healed (Num 21:4–9).

Many years later Jesus used that incident as a picture of his death and its effects.

'As Moses lifted up the bronze snake on a pole in the desert, in the same way the Son of Man must be lifted up, so that everyone who believes in him may have eternal life' John 3:14–15.

THE WATER TEST

'Why did you bring us here? There is not even any water to drink!'

The people were grumbling at Moses and Aaron again. God told Moses to assemble the whole community in front of a large rock and to speak to the rock. God promised to make water flow out of the rock. But Moses struck the rock and said angrily, 'Do we have to get water out of this rock for you?'

Because Moses disobeyed God and also took the credit for providing the water, neither he nor Aaron were allowed to lead the Israelites into the Promised Land (Numbers 20:1–13).

From the top of Mount Nebo God showed Moses the Promised Land of Canaan which the Israelites were to claim.

NEW LEADERS

Moses was a good leader but he found the responsibility for so many people too much to handle on his own. God authorised him to choose seventy respected men to share the task (Num 11:10–17).

When it came time for the Israelites to enter the land of Canaan, two people were appointed to succeed Moses and Aaron. They were Joshua, who had been Moses' assistant, and Eleazar, Aaron's son, who became High Priest. Along with representatives from each of the twelve tribes, they would divide the land for the people.

In the book of Deuteronomy Moses makes his final speech to the people. He reminds them of what God has done for them. He reminds them again of God's laws. And he reminds them that they have to choose between obeying God and disobeying him; between blessing and unhappiness (Deut 30:15–20).

TODAY

Our choice today is the same as that given by Moses to the people:

'Today I am giving you a choice between good and evil, between life and death' (Deut 30:15)

JOSHUA
FORWARD INTO BATTLE

1300 BC	1250	1200
/JOSHUA	/ENTRY TO CANAAN	

The book of Joshua is not just the story of great events in the life of a great leader. It shows how God used Joshua to keep a promise made several centuries before to Abraham (Genesis 15: 12–21). Now was the time for God's people to occupy the land of Canaan and settle in it.

JOSHUA – AN ABLE LEADER
Moses never entered the Promised Land. However, before he died he appointed someone well qualified to lead God's people across the River Jordan (Deut 31:1–8). If a report had been written about Joshua it might have included the following comments:

☐ **Battle skills** Joshua has been very successful in this subject. Under his leadership the Israelites defeated a band of desert warriors. The full story is in Exodus 17:8–13.

☐ **Life skills** Joshua has responded well to Moses' instruction ever since he was young (Numbers 11:28).

☐ **Religious education** Joshua has shown trust in God's power. Moses sent spies to explore Canaan, and most of them came back terrified by the strength and size of the people already in the land (Numbers 13:31–33). Only two spies, Joshua and Caleb, believed God was able to give them the land.

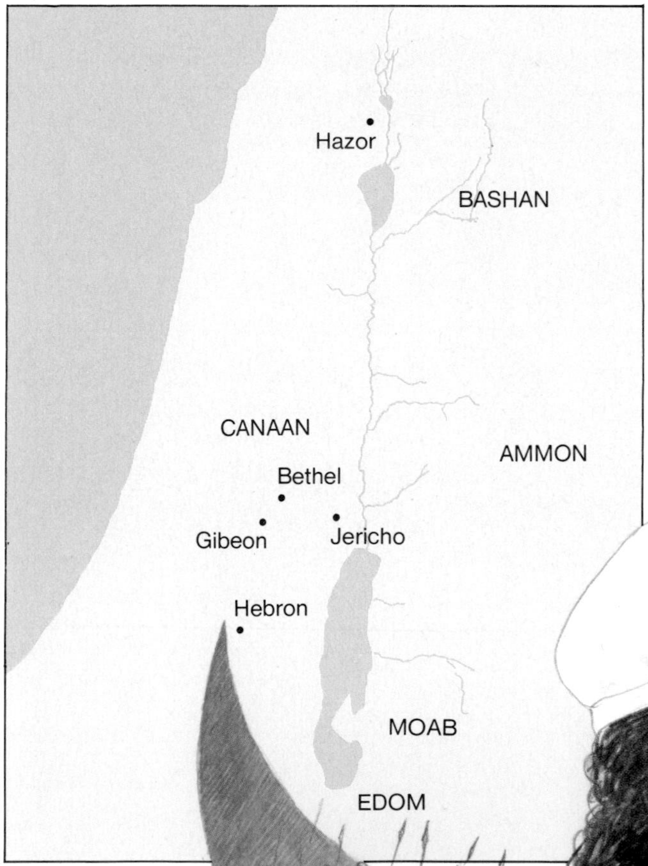

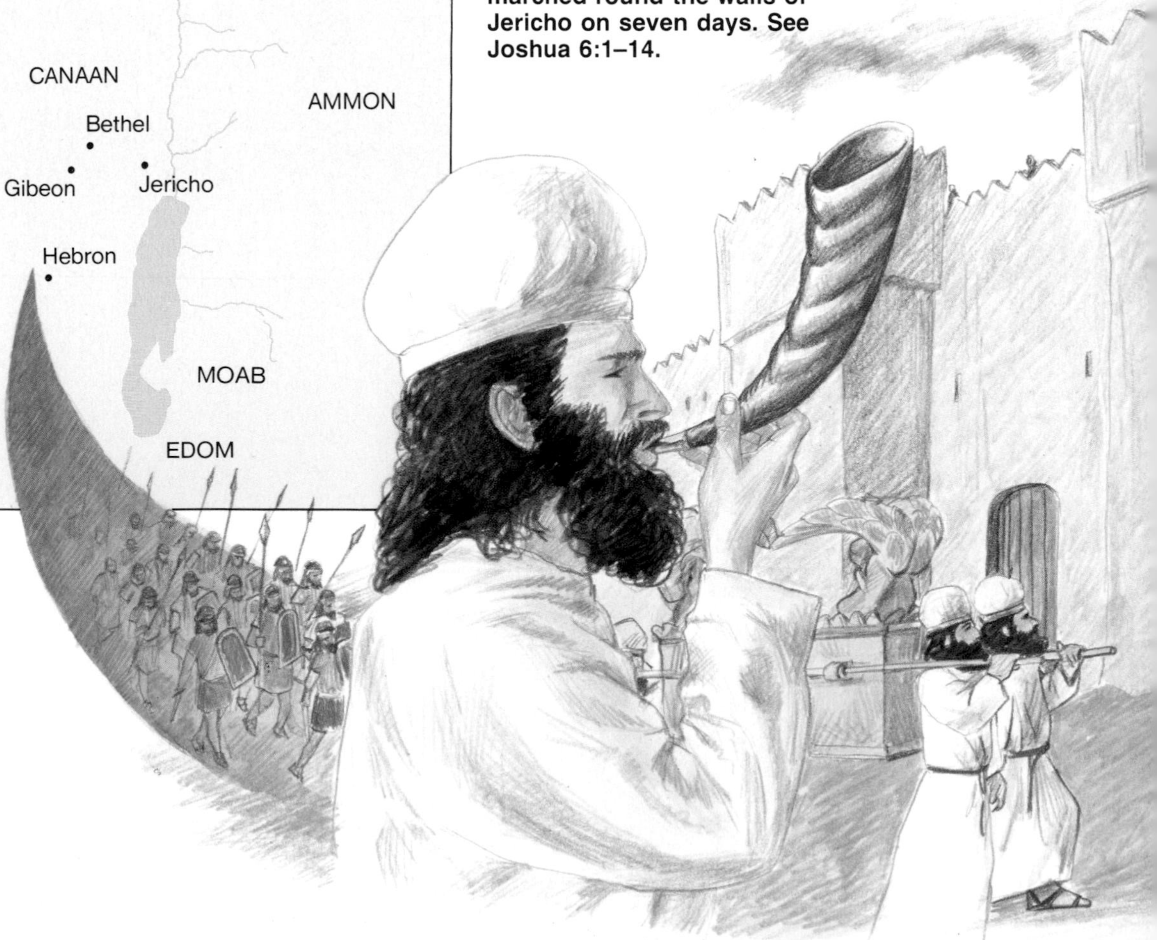

Hazor

BASHAN

CANAAN

Bethel

Gibeon   Jericho

AMMON

Hebron

MOAB

EDOM

A procession of Israelite soldiers, priests carrying the Covenant Box and others blowing trumpets marched round the walls of Jericho on seven days. See Joshua 6:1–14.

All of these qualifications were important, but in the end it was God's call that marked out Joshua as leader. With it came a tremendous promise (Joshua 1:9).

'AND THE WALLS FELL TUMBLING DOWN'

Joshua did not need to fight to take Jericho. The people of Jericho doubtless thought they were safe behind their massive walls and laughed at the trumpet-blowing Israelites marching round the city every day. But they had not reckoned with the power of Israel's God (Joshua 6:1–9). Only the faithful Rahab and her family were spared when the Israelites stormed over the ruined wall (Josh 6:20–25). God's people had captured their first city in the Promised Land in an amazing way. No wonder Joshua's 'fame spread through the whole country' (Josh 6:27).

GOD'S CLEAR INSTRUCTIONS

God commanded Joshua to invade the land of Canaan and kill those he defeated. Defeat was God's way of punishing the Canaanites for their evil practices. The destruction that followed was also to protect God's people. If they were to start worshipping Canaanite gods they would be punished as well (Judges 2:2–3).

MISSION ACCOMPLISHED?

The first twelve chapters of the Book of Joshua show how successful the Israelites were in destroying the Canaanites and in taking their land. Read Joshua 11:16, for example. However, when Joshua was very old, and even after his death, there was 'still much land to be taken' (Joshua 13:1, Judges 1:1). The army had won many important victories when the land was first invaded, but these had to be followed up by a more thorough conquest as the tribes began to settle down and build their homes (Judges 1:3). In fact the conquest was never completed, and the Israelites accepted that some Canaanites would remain in the land (Judges 1:27– 35).

WE WILL SERVE THE LORD!

When Joshua was very old he called a meeting of Israelites. He reminded them of the ways in which God had led them and been faithful to them (Joshua 24:1–13). Now they must decide whether they would be faithful to God or not. They shouldn't say 'yes' lightly because God would punish them if they turned away from him to worship other gods. Joshua knew what *he* would do: 'As for my family and me, we will serve the Lord' (Joshua 24:15). When the people promised to be obedient, an agreement, or covenant, was made and recorded (Joshua 24:24– 27).

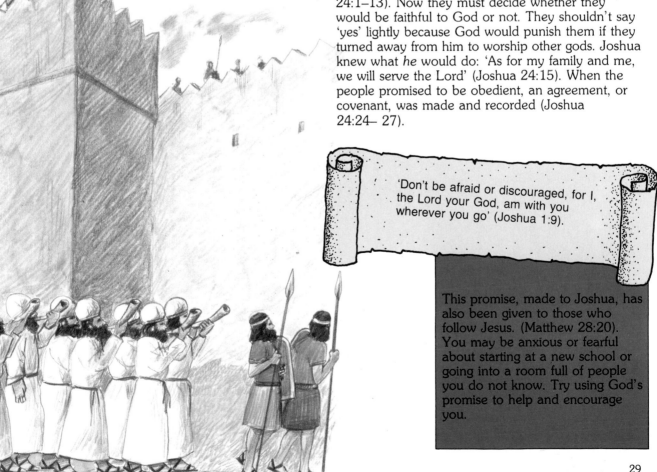

'Don't be afraid or discouraged, for I, the Lord your God, am with you wherever you go' (Joshua 1:9).

This promise, made to Joshua, has also been given to those who follow Jesus. (Matthew 28:20). You may be anxious or fearful about starting at a new school or going into a room full of people you do not know. Try using God's promise to help and encourage you.

THE CANAANITES

A GREAT DISCOVERY

In the spring of 1928 a Syrian farmer was pushing a wooden-handled plough over his field when he struck what looked like a tombstone. Within a few months archaeologists had discovered twenty clay tablets buried in the nearby mound of Ugarit. On the tablets were wedge-shaped notches, known as cuneiform writing. Later hundreds more were uncovered in a room which used to be a library.

These provided a lot of information about the people of Canaan amongst whom the Israelites settled over 3000 years ago.

Inside the palace at Ugarit were found many pictures carved on ivory panels. One of these panels, over a metre wide, originally formed the foot of the royal bedstead.

Canaanite jewellery.

CANAANITE RELIGION

The Canaanites worshipped a great number of gods, and the Ugarit tablets record a rich variety of stories about their gods' love affairs, parties, and battles. If they led such hectic lives, the gods could not have had much time to be interested in mere humans. They hardly seem the sort of gods you could trust in, and yet many Israelites were tempted to do so. There were two main reasons:

☐ **Weather** To grow crops the Canaanites needed water, but for much of the year the land was dry. Unless there was enough rain during the wet winter months, when the crops grew, people would die of starvation. The Canaanites believed they would suffer if they did not please 'good' gods like Baal, who supposedly had the power to make rainstorms. When the Israelites settled in Canaan, they copied Canaanite methods of cultivating the land, and they were tempted to worship their gods as well.

☐ **Lifestyle** The Israelite God demanded very high standards of behaviour, but drunkenness and adultery were positively encouraged at Canaanite festivals. It was easier for the Israelites to copy the Canaanite way of life but it caused them a lot of trouble, as we will see when we look at the Judges.

JUDGES
DEBORAH, GIDEON, SAMSON AND RUTH

1200 BC	1150	1100

THE JUDGES

Baal, the most popular of the Canaanite gods.

'There was no king in Israel at that time. Everyone did just as he pleased' (Judges 21:25).

That is how the writer of the Book of Judges sums up the period following the invasion of Canaan. The Israelites disobeyed God's laws, and idol-worship became common.

We think of a judge today as someone who sits in court making legal decisions. But in Israel judges were warrior-leaders whom God used to win amazing victories. Their special place in God's plan can be seen in the chart below.

1. The Israelites worshipped other gods. (Judges 2:12,19)

2. God allowed surrounding nations to attack the Israelites. (Judges 2:14)

3. The people begged God to forgive and rescue them. (Judges 2:18)

Each sequence led the people deeper into sin (Judges 2:19). Look at Judges 3:7–12 to see this pattern of events in connection with the first judge, Othniel.

5. The judge died. (Judges 2:19)

4. God provided a judge, who defeated the enemy in battle. (Judges 2:18)

IS IT ALL TOO EASY FOR US?

In our country today we do not have to worry so much about the size of the harvest or whether there will be one. Irrigation, fertilisers, and new methods of farming reduce our dependence on nature, and few of us are involved in farming anyway. We are made to feel secure in other ways as well. When we are children we have parents or friends to make sure we are fed and have enough clothes and later on we can use insurance policies to reduce the loss caused by an accident or theft. If we are ill the state or a health insurance scheme provides for us, and there are many other organisations to help those in need. The danger for us is not that we will chase after foreign gods but that we will not feel the need for God at all.

A team of combine harvesters at work.

DEBORAH
A JUDGE WITH AUTHORITY

GIDEON
A RELUCTANT JUDGE

CANAANITES With his nine hundred iron chariots King Jabin was able to control the flat coastal plain. (Judges 4:3)

MIDIANITES These and other desert tribes used camels to make frequent raids. They snatched the harvest from the Israelites to increase their own food supply (Judges 6:1–6).

When the Israelites began to worship other gods (yet again!), the Lord used Jabin, a Canaanite king, to punish them. For twenty years there was great suffering in the land because of Jabin's cruelty, but at last the people begged God to help them (Judges 4:1–3). The victory that followed was inspired by the judge, Deborah, but was a clear sign of God's strength. She ordered Barak to march with a large army of foot soldiers to the top of a hill overlooking a wide plain. As the dreaded Canaanite chariots approached, Deborah ordered the army to charge down the hillside. An unexpected rainstorm turned the plain into a bog in which the chariots became stuck, and before long many were being washed away by the river in flood (Judges 4:4–16). Afterwards Deborah and Barak sang a song, praising God for the victory (Judges 5).

An excerpt from Gideon's diary:
'I told God I wasn't the right person to choose if he wanted to deliver Israel from the raiding Midianites. After all, I am the least important member of the weakest tribe. What kind of leader would that make me, I asked.

'I needed a lot of convincing that it really was God giving me instructions, but then I made sure to gather as large an army as I could. It was still far smaller than the enemy force, which was like a swarm of locusts in the valley. But God thought it was far too big. He told me the Israelites might think they had won by themselves and not give God the credit. I had to use extraordinary tests to reduce my army to a mere three hundred men.

'That night I was totally convinced of God's unlimited power. A few strange noises in the night were enough to make the enemy panic and kill each other in the confusion. All I had to do was to use my handful of men to mop up what was left.' (Judges 6 and 7).

'They might think that they had won by themselves' (Judges 7:2).

'Listen! The noisy crowds round the walls are telling of the Lord's victories, the victories of Israel's people!' (Judges 5:11).

DIARY OF A TEENAGER

Thursday 20

I'm being interviewed at Youth Club tonight about how I became a Christian at camp and what difference it's made to me. I've felt weak-kneed at the thought because I don't find speaking in front of others easy.
BUT — I've just read about Gideon's soldiers. They found that it was in their weakness that God's power could best be shown. That's helped me a lot because I know God can help me to do my best, and that's all he wants of me

SETTLING IN A NEW LAND

SAMSON
A LONER

PHILISTINES Known as 'Sea peoples', they gained control over much of Israel's territory as well as the southern coastlands. The armour shows their skill at metalwork.

Samson was the most exciting of the judges. The story of his life is in Judges 13–16. Repeatedly, when something made him angry, he attacked large numbers of the Philistines single-handed (Judges 14:19–20) and lions were certainly no match for him (Judg 14:5–6). The enemy failed to capture him until the secret of his power was discovered by his girlfriend. When his hair was cut, the Nazirite vow made for him by his parents was broken, and his strength was lost. Blinded and put in chains he was made to grind corn. Later, during a big festival, the Philistine kings called for Samson to entertain them. By then his hair had grown again and, as he pulled the building down on top of them all, 'he killed more people at his death than he had killed during his life' (Judg 16:4–30).

MISTAKES
BUT NOT FAILURES

The wrong-doings of the judges were not covered up; read Judges 8:27 and 16:1, for example. However, because of their faith the judges were able to achieve a lot (Hebrews 11:32–34). Similarly, God does not think we are failures just because we are sometimes in the wrong.

RUTH
A STORY OF FAMILY LOYALTY

After the troubles and violence of the judges, the book of Ruth tells a peaceful family story. During the time of the judges there was a shortage of food in Israel and many people left. One family settled in neighbouring Moab but the father and two sons died. The mother, Naomi, decided to return to Israel. One of her daughters-in-law, Ruth, was very fond of Naomi and left her home country of Moab to settle in Israel with her. They arrived in Bethlehem as poor widows, but God provided a relative, Boaz, to look after them. Boaz and Ruth were married and had a son who was the ancestor of both King David and Jesus.

Boaz was a farmer, and it was during the barley harvest that he first met Ruth who went into his fields to glean grain.

Threshing Sheaves were taken to the threshing floor, where the grain was freed from the stalks by an ox-drawn thresher. At night the grain had to be protected from thieves and wild animals. (3:6–7)

Winnowing The threshed wheat was tossed into the air to let unwanted chaff blow away.

Gleaning Reapers were forbidden to go back over a field to collect grain they had missed. This gave poor people like Ruth a chance to pick up, or glean, what remained. (2:1–3)

Reaping Grain was cut with a sickle and bound into sheaves by a team of reapers. (Ruth 2:8–9)

33

1 SAMUEL

JUDGE AND PROPHET

1100 BC   1050   1000

/SAMUEL

'When Samuel spoke, all Israel listened' (1 Samuel 3:21)

The first book of Samuel tells the story of a man with a special part to play in Israel's history as the last of the judges and a prophet. Even his birth was special, as the story in 1 Samuel 1 shows. Keeping the promise she had made (1:22), Hannah presented the boy, Samuel, to the priest Eli. He was to be Eli's helper in the Temple, which was in Shiloh at that time (1 Sam 2:19–22).

One night, when Samuel was still a boy, God told him how he was going to punish Eli and his family for doing wrong. As he grew up Samuel was also told by God to warn the people of the disasters that would soon overwhelm them. True to his word, Israel was defeated by the Philistines in battle, the treasured Covenant Box (see page 40) was captured, Eli and his sons were punished, and Shiloh was utterly destroyed (1 Sam 4:10–18, Jeremiah 7:12–15). Samuel was therefore judge during a critical period in Israel's history. Before long the people were looking for a new way out of their troubles.

'WE WANT A KING'

THE REQUEST OF THE ISRAELITES
'Give us a king to rule over us. We don't want Samuel's sons as our so-called leaders. You know how often they bend the rules. We want to be like everyone else and have a king. Then we will always have someone to help us fight our enemies.'

Beitin (Bethel) was one of the places on Samuel's circuit as a judge.

SAMUEL ADDRESSES THE CROWD
'Fellow Israelites, you are making a serious mistake in asking for a king. You will be forced to work for the king. You will have to pay taxes to meet the king's bills, and some of you will even become his slaves. When this happens you will have only yourselves to blame.'

GOD'S REPLY, GIVEN TO SAMUEL
'I wanted them to be people I could trust, but instead of treating me as king they have ignored me. They have worshipped the gods of other nations and now they want to copy them by having a human king. They must be warned where it will lead them.'

SAMUEL ANOINTS SAUL
'The people have demanded a king, and the Lord is anointing you to rule his people and protect them from all his enemies.'

1 AND 2 SAMUEL
KING SAUL AND KING DAVID

1050 BC	1000	950
/SAUL	/DAVID	

SAUL
ISRAEL'S FIRST KING

(1 Sam 13:14).

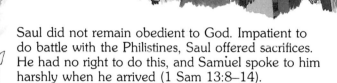

BECAUSE YOU HAVE DISOBEYED HIM, THE LORD WILL FIND THE KIND OF MAN HE WANTS AND MAKE HIM RULER OF HIS PEOPLE

Saul made an impressive start. Enemy Ammonites agreed to make peace with some Israelites only if they had their right eyes gouged out. Horrified at these terms, Saul gathered a large army in a most unusual way and won a victory that saved God's people from an awful fate (1 Sam 11:1–15).

Saul did not remain obedient to God. Impatient to do battle with the Philistines, Saul offered sacrifices. He had no right to do this, and Samuel spoke to him harshly when he arrived (1 Sam 13:8–14).

On another occasion Saul disobeyed God and Samuel warned him. Saul grasped hold of Samuel's cloak, and it ripped. 'So the Lord has torn the kingdom of Israel away from you today,' said the prophet (1 Sam 15:1–33).

David was privately anointed king, and his fame as a warrior spread quickly. Saul became jealous, and in a fit of rage threw his spear at David. Eventually David was forced to flee from Saul's palace (1 Sam 18:6–15; 19:9–12).

To have David in exile was not enough. Saul wanted him dead. Neglecting the threat of the Philistines, Saul chased his hated enemy through barren wastelands, but without success (1 Sam 23:25–29).

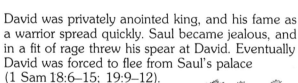

In danger of being crushed by the powerful Philistine army, Saul became desperate. He tried to get help by calling up the spirit of Samuel (1 Sam 28:7–19), but he could not avoid death at the hands of the enemy (1 Sam 31:1–7).

A FRESH START
Saul's life seemed so full of promise, but one sin led to another. His problem is sometimes ours too. For example, when we tell one lie we are often forced to tell another one later. The way out is to own up, say sorry, and ask forgiveness. With God's help we can then make a fresh start (1 John 1:8–9).

DAVID
THE IDEAL KING

David was considered by some to be the ideal king, but he had his faults too. If there had been a televised discussion after his death it might have gone like this:

David was a great king because he knew the importance of finding out what God wanted him to do. While he was being chased through the wilderness he twice had Saul at his mercy, but refused to harm him. He believed that when it was time for him to be king God himself would dispose of Saul (1 Sam 24:1–22, 26:1–12). Even after Saul's death David did not immediately march to claim the throne. He asked God for guidance (2 Samuel 2:1).

David made sure that his people were always treated fairly and justly (2 Samuel 8:15).

Yes, he certainly timed things well. Like when he invited the lovely Bathsheba to the palace while her husband was fighting his battles for him. Very timely! So was her husband's death. David thought no one would discover how well planned it was (2 Sam 11:1–27).

True, but at least he didn't take offence when God punished him. Remember his response, 'Be merciful to me, O God, because of your constant love . . . Wash away all my evil and make me clean from my sin. I recognize my faults' (Psalm 51:1–3). Not many kings would have said that.

David showed he was a shrewd leader by capturing Jerusalem and building his capital there:

- He captured the hill-town from the Jebusites, so no-one could accuse him of favouring a particular tribe by building on their land.
- It was an excellent defensive site. No wonder the Jebusites mocked as David's men approached. How clever David's tactics were! Using that water tunnel took the guards by surprise (2 Sam 5:6–10).
- Once the ark had been carried into the city, Jerusalem was the religious as well as the political capital of Israel (2 Sam 6:12–15).

You say he was a shrewd leader. Why then didn't he bring up his children better? By failing to punish his son Amnon for dreadful misbehaviour David infuriated another son, Absalom (2 Sam 13:1–33). Absalom was determined to replace David as king, and stirred up a Civil War. When the rebels were finally defeated all David could do was cry over the death of his son. This was no way of showing thanks to his supporters, and David's army leader ordered him to stop making a fool of himself (2 Sam 19:1–8). Failing to learn the lesson, David put off making a decision about which son would succeed him and caused unnecessary trouble (1 Kings 1:5–35).

David wasn't perfect, but his love for God, and his deep desire to serve him, can be seen in the songs he wrote. Many people have found David's Psalms help them greatly in worship. Psalm 23 is often a favourite, with its opening lines, 'The Lord is my shepherd; I have everything I need. He lets me rest in fields of green grass and leads me to quiet pools of fresh water' (verses 1–2). When God's people were in trouble later on they remembered God's promise that David's kingdom would last for ever (2 Sam 7:16). They looked to the future with new

hope, waiting for the Messiah, who would be a descendant of David (Isaiah 55:3–4).

THE REIGN OF SOLOMON

1000 BC	950	900
/DAVID	/SOLOMON	

THE KINGS: SUCCESS OR FAILURE

The books of Kings continue the history of the Israelite kings begun in the books of Samuel. The kings are not judged by their military strength or by their wealth, as in most history books; only if they were loyal to God are they considered by the writer to have been successful.

The first book of Kings begins with the reign of Solomon, who was David's son by Bathsheba.

WHAT A DREAM!

'What would you like me to give you?' How would we answer if God asked us this? King Solomon's reply was: 'Give me the wisdom I need to rule your people with justice and to know the difference between good and evil' (1 Kings 3:9). This answer pleased God so much that Solomon was promised other things as well, including great wealth and honour (1 Kings 3:4–14).

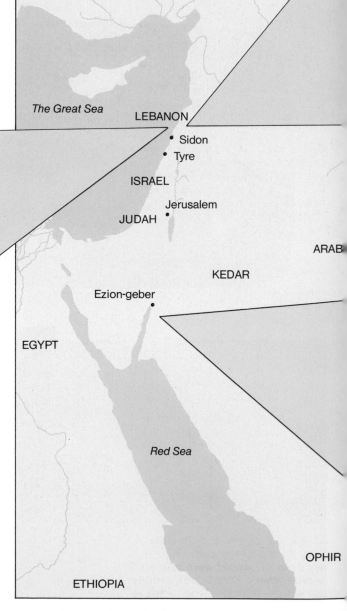

A Phoenician boat. Solomon depended greatly on the skills of Phoenicians for his sea trade (1 Kings 9:26–28).

The Great Sea

LEBANON
• Sidon
• Tyre

ISRAEL

Jerusalem
JUDAH •

ARAB

KEDAR

Ezion-geber •

EGYPT

Red Sea

OPHIR

ETHIOPIA

SOLOMON'S WISDOM

Through his fairness in settling arguments Solomon won the respect of God's people. They would always remember how he threatened to cut a baby in half to solve a particularly difficult case. See 1 Kings 3:16–28. He also became famous for his proverbs, songs and psalms, and for his deep understanding of nature (1 Kings 4:29–34). Even the Queen of Sheba was amazed when she saw how easily Solomon could answer all her questions and riddles (1 Kings 10:1–9).

SOLOMON'S WEALTH

Just as God had promised, Solomon became fabulously rich. By well-planned marriages with foreign women Solomon was able to make his kingdom bigger and more powerful. Taxes paid by Israel's colonies were a useful source of money.

However, Solomon's riches were gained mainly through trade. A lot of money could be made through buying cheaply and selling elsewhere at a much higher price. Solomon had great success in selling to his neighbours horses from Turkey and chariots from Egypt (1 Kings 10:28, 29).

Solomon's kingdom was so large that he had ports on both the Mediterranean and Red Seas. Copper mined and smelted near Ezion Geber was traded for gold from Ophir. By shipping direct he was able to cut out Arabian overland trade. Doubtless the Queen of Sheba did not come all the way from southern Arabia just to flatter Solomon; she also hoped to gain a better deal for her traders.

The major land trade routes between Egypt and Asia passed through Israel. Taxation of the traders provided more money for the treasury (1 Kings 10:15).

Cedar trees were felled in Lebanon, dragged down to the sea and floated along the coast. Cedar beams and boards were used in the temple and in the king's palace (1 Kings 5:8–9).

At the foot of these cliffs were King Solomon's mines. The deposits of copper were refined nearby where the northerly winds fanned the flames of the furnace.

MONEY NO OBJECT

Solomon became so wealthy that silver was as common as stone in Jerusalem (1 Kings 10:27). His household lived in style. Thirty cows and a hundred sheep were slaughtered every day to feed them; and the menu was varied with regular supplies of deer, gazelles, roebucks and poultry.

The majority of Solomon's budget was spent on an ambitious building programme. To improve the security of his kingdom he strengthened the defences of cities on its border, and stables were built for twelve thousand cavalry horses (1 Kings 10:26). The biggest changes, however, were in Jerusalem. The king's new palace was so splendid with its huge stones and cedar beams that it took thirteen years to build (1 Kings 7:1–12).

The magnificent temple was Solomon's greatest achievement (see pages 40/41).

THE COST OF SOLOMON'S WEALTH

Samuel had warned the people how kings would treat them (see page 34). In Solomon's reign the prophecy was fulfilled. Thousands were sent to help transport cedar logs from Lebanon (1 Kings 5:9), while others had to quarry limestone and cut it into blocks up to ten metres long (1 Kings 5:13–18). No wonder the people promised to support Solomon's successor only if he did not treat them as badly (1 Kings 12:4).

Solomon's policy of marrying foreign women also had a high cost. With the wives came foreign religions, and Solomon did not remain faithful to God. He worshipped other gods and even built places where they could be worshipped. Punishment was bound to follow (1 Kings 11:1–13).

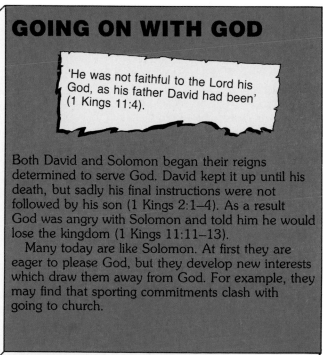

GOING ON WITH GOD

'He was not faithful to the Lord his God, as his father David had been' (1 Kings 11:4).

Both David and Solomon began their reigns determined to serve God. David kept it up until his death, but sadly his final instructions were not followed by his son (1 Kings 2:1–4). As a result God was angry with Solomon and told him he would lose the kingdom (1 Kings 11:11–13).

Many today are like Solomon. At first they are eager to please God, but they develop new interests which draw them away from God. For example, they may find that sporting commitments clash with going to church.

SOLOMON'S TEMPLE

> *NOW I HAVE BUILT A MAJESTIC TEMPLE FOR YOU, A PLACE FOR YOU TO LIVE IN FOR EVER*
> *(1 Kings 8:13).*

David wanted to build a temple but God told him that his son, Solomon, should build it instead. Solomon used the best materials and employed expert craftsmen, and it took seven years to complete the temple.

Types of offering

What have victory in war, a careless promise and awareness of a wrong action got in common? All were occasions when sacrifices should be offered in the temple. Detailed instructions about the nature of the offering and how it should be dealt with are given in the Book of Leviticus. Poor people who could not afford animals were allowed to bring birds or even flour (Lev 5:7–13), but any offering had to be without defect; only the best would do (Lev 1:3). (See page 25)

Sacrifices were offered to thank God for his goodness. They were also God's way of dealing with sin.

He wanted to show that wrong-doing grieved him. Instead of punishing the wrong-doer, God accepted from him the sacrifice of an animal and the person knew it was being killed instead of him. These sacrifices led up to the one perfect sacrifice of Jesus Christ on the cross. (See page 91)

Sacrifice alone was not enough; prayer was also central to temple worship. At the opening ceremony of the temple, Solomon repeatedly asked the Lord to hear the humble prayers of his people. (1 Kings 8:30–55) Sadly, it was not always treated as a 'house of prayer' (Mark 11:17).

1. Holy of Holies

Inside the dark, windowless room stood Israel's most holy object – the Covenant Box (1 Kings 6:19–28). This movable gold-coated chest contained the tablets of the law given to Moses. On the lid were two cherubim, winged creatures with human faces. The Box was thought of as the earthly throne of God himself. Therefore only the High Priest was allowed into the Holy of Holies, and only once a year when he made an offering on behalf of all God's people (Hebrews 9:3–7).

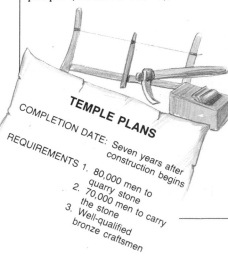

TEMPLE PLANS

COMPLETION DATE: Seven years after construction begins

REQUIREMENTS 1. 80,000 men to quarry stone

2. 70,000 men to carry the stone

3. Well-qualified bronze craftsmen

2. Storerooms

Used to store offerings and some of the priests' clothes, they also housed the temple treasury. In one of these little rooms an important discovery was later to be made (2 Chronicles 34:14).

3. Bronze basins

A huge basin, four and a half metres in diameter, was used by the priests to purify themselves by washing. Ten wheeled carts supported smaller basins in which the sacrifices were washed (1 Kings 7:23–39).

4. The Holy Place

From the entrance hall, beautifully carved doors opened into the largest room in the temple. Only a little light penetrated the small windows high in the wall, but it

was enough to see the gleam of gold-coated carvings on the walls and gold furnishings. There were five pairs of candlesticks, a small altar on which sweet-smelling perfume was constantly burnt, and a table on which twelve loaves were kept (1 Kings 7:48–50).

5. Priests and Levites

The tribe of Levi had been appointed during Moses' lifetime to have special religious duties. (See page 23) Once the temple had been built, many Levites served there as porters and doorkeepers, or sang in one of the temple choirs.

Only those who were descendants of the Levite Aaron could become priests (Numbers 3:5–10). Their main tasks were to pray and to offer sacrifices on behalf of the people. The High

Priest had extra responsibilities. On the breastplate of his gown, called an ephod, was a pouch. This contained the Urim and Thummim which were used to find out what decision God wanted (Num 27:21). Possibly they were two flat objects, one of which would be drawn out, rather like tossing a coin today.

6. Altar
A large structure, more than twice the height of a man, on which sacrifices were burnt.

MODERN CHURCHES

The temple was the earthly home of God in which he made his presence known in a very special way. Hence the luxurious fittings provided by Solomon. Most people stayed in the courtyard to worship so the temple building did not need to be large. Indeed, being only thirty metres long, it was smaller than many of our local churches.

Today God makes his presence known in Christian people, through the Holy Spirit, rather than in a building. The role of a church is therefore as a centre for Christian worship.

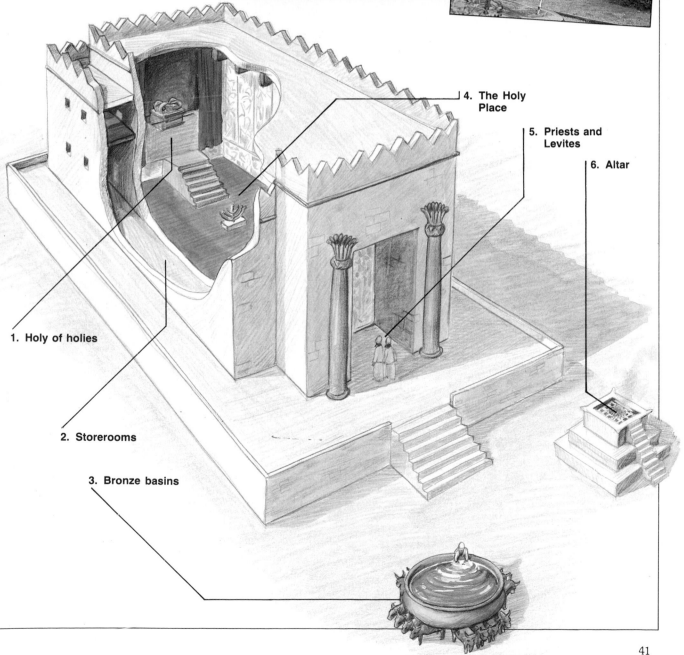

4. **The Holy Place**

5. **Priests and Levites**

6. **Altar**

1. **Holy of holies**

2. **Storerooms**

3. **Bronze basins**

ONE NATION BECOMES TWO

The Jewish nation became firmly established as a kingdom under David, but now it reaches a difficult time in its history. King Solomon, David's successor to the throne, marries many foreign women, who bring their false gods along too – and the Jews begin to worship them rather than the true God. God warns Solomon that he will take most of the nation away from his successor, but Solomon ignores God's warning.

When Solomon dies there are two people who want to be king – Rehoboam, his son and heir, and Jeroboam, a clever man who had worked for Solomon. Solomon had tried to kill him when he heard it said that God was going to give Jeroboam ten of the Jewish tribes to rule over. Jeroboam escaped to Egypt, where he lived until Solomon died. Rehoboam is officially declared King, but Jeroboam returns from Egypt, and goes to him along with the leaders of the ten northern tribes to present a petition.

Sadly, instead of giving them what they ask for, as his older, wiser advisors tell him to, Rehoboam takes notice of a group of his young friends. You can read about this in I Kings chapter 12, verses 1–17.

I AM GOING TO MAKE LIFE EVEN HARDER FOR YOU.

So the nation becomes divided. The ten northern tribes become the Kingdom of Israel, and Jeroboam is made their king. The two southern tribes of Judah and Benjamin become the Kingdom of Judah, and remain loyal to King Rehoboam.

IS GOD REALLY IN CHARGE?

It must have looked as if everything was going from bad to worse in the Jewish nation. God had promised there would always be a descendant of David on the throne in Jerusalem – what would happen now? Rehoboam is David's grandson so David's descendants still rule. Although only two tribes remain loyal, large numbers of people are not necessary to God for the carrying out of his will. We see often in the Bible and the history of Christianity how he uses just a few people to bring about his plans.

2 KINGS

ELIJAH AND ELISHA
BOLD MEN WHO STOOD UP FOR GOD'S TRUTH

900 BC	800	700

/KINGDOM DIVIDED /ELIJAH /ELISHA

According to the writer of the Book of Kings, all the kings of the northern kingdom of Israel behaved wickedly, but one of the worst was Ahab, and his foreign wife, Jezebel, who taught the Israelites to worship Baal – a foreign god whom she said could control the weather. God sends Elijah at this critical moment to tell them he is angry at their false worship. He will show by a long drought that it is God and not Baal who controls the weather. Elijah is hated by Ahab and Jezebel as a result.

Elijah is protected from the effects of the drought, and his faith strengthened, as he sees God providing for his basic needs of food and drink. You can read how God worked a miracle to make food last in I Kings chapter 17: 8–16.

At the end of three years Elijah arranges a contest between four hundred priests of Baal and himself, to prove to the Israelites who is the true God. 1 Kings 18 tells us about the dramatic challenge on Mount Carmel. Afterwards Elijah escapes into the desert to avoid being assassinated by angry Jezebel. Some time later, Elijah is sent back by God to continue challenging Ahab's conscience.

Elijah's message to King Ahab: 'In the name of the Lord . . . whom I serve, I tell you that there will be no dew or rain for the next two or three years until I say so!

When Elijah is taken up to heaven in a fiery chariot, his servant Elisha inherits his God-given power, continuing to remind the nation of God's truth, and how he wants them to live. He performs miracles, like Elijah before him – an account of these can be found in chapters 2–5 of II Kings; the best known of all involved the Syrian army commander Naaman, who was healed of leprosy.

NAAMAN'S CURE
Naaman hears about Elisha from a Jewish slave girl. Elisha could heal him!

Elisha's servant tells Naaman, 'Go and wash in The River Jordan seven times.'

Naaman is angry and refuses to do it. 'Elisha could at least tell me himself.'

He is finally persuaded by his servants to try it, and is healed. 'The leprosy's gone!'

Elijah and Elisha were not very popular with the wicked people of their time, but that did not stop them urging people to live by God's standards. Today we do not have prophets quite like Elijah and Elisha but there are people who, in different ways, encourage and lead others to live by God's standards. Abraham Lincoln, Dietrich Bonhoeffer and Lord Shaftesbury are famous for their bold stand for justice.

EXILE

The books of 1 and 2 Kings and 1 and 2 Chronicles can make complicated reading! The lists of the kings of Israel and Judah are used to record important events, eg 'In the third year of King 'so- and-so' of Judah, King 'such-and- such' of Israel died.' Things began to go wrong in the northern kingdom of Israel. Here is what happened.

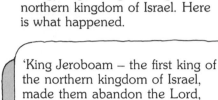

'King Jeroboam – the first king of the northern kingdom of Israel, made them abandon the Lord, and led them into terrible sins' (2 Kings 17:21).

They also made an image of the goddess Asherah, worshipped the stars, and served the god Baal (2 Kings 17: 16).

'He made two golden bulls to worship, and set up altars in Dan and Bethel' – God had said they were not to use statues in worship.

They sacrificed their sons and daughters as burnt offerings to pagan gods (2 Kings 17: 17).

They consulted mediums and fortune tellers and they devoted themselves completely to doing what is wrong in the Lord's sight (2 Kings 17: 17).

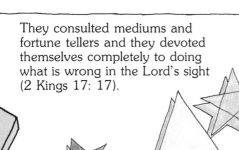

... SO GOD SPOKE TO THEM ...

The Lord sent his messengers and prophets to warn Israel – but they would not obey; they were stubborn (2 Kings 17: 13 & 14).

The Lord was angry with the Israelites, and banished them from his sight – this happened in 722 BC, when the Assyrian King Sennacherib invaded Samaria, the capital of Israel, and took the Israelites away to Assyria as captives, leaving only the southern kingdom of Judah (2 Kings 17: 18).

BUT

Even the people of Judah did not obey God's laws – they imitated the people of Israel (2 Kings 17: 19–20). Two hundred years later, Jerusalem was destroyed, and they were taken prisoners to Babylon.

HISTORY CHECK-LIST

ISRAEL

- ☐ No continuous royal line.
- ☐ Frequent rebellions.
- ☐ One bad king after another.
- ☐ Abandoned, almost totally, the worship of God.
- ☐ Samaria, the capital, destroyed by Sennacherib, King of Assyria in 722 BC; Israelites taken captive to Assyria.

JUDAH

- ☐ Managed to keep the royal line intact.
- ☐ Three outstanding good kings, Uzziah, Hezekiah, Josiah, helped the people to return to a more pure form of worship.
- ☐ Remained more faithful in worship of God.
- ☐ Jerusalem destroyed by King Nebuchadnezzar in 587 BC: people of Judah taken captive to Babylon.

Have God's plans for his people failed? The ten northern tribes mingled and disappeared in Assyria, and were never heard of again, but the people of Judah stayed together as a group, and finally returned to Jerusalem – the royal family line still intact. In spite of man's disobedience and wickedness, God carries out the plans he has made.

God has made good plans for us as individuals, as well as for whole groups of people. We need to understand God's teaching from the Bible, so that we can cooperate with God in bringing them about.

To see how God carries out his plans in spite of set-backs, read the story of Gladys Aylward who was turned down by the missionary society she applied to, yet became one of the best known missionaries of this century.

THE LAND BETWEEN THE TWO RIVERS

The Jews were taken captive to Babylonia, also known as 'The Land between the Two Rivers' (Tigris and Euphrates). Babylonia had conquered many nations and was the major world power at the time. The city of Babylon was famous for its fine buildings and gardens.

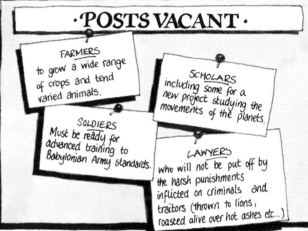

JEWISH EXILES' GUIDE TO BABYLON

Change is always hard – you've plenty to adjust to here!

CLIMATE	Hot and humid; the whole country is a low-lying plain between the rivers Tigris and Euphrates (very different from our Palestinian hills!)
RELIGION	(Or religions – there seem so many!) The Babylonians worship the sun, the moon, and lots of fertility gods.
BUILDINGS WORTH SEEING	The Hanging Gardens of Babylon, internationally famous palace built by King Nebuchadnezzar for his wife, with lush gardens on terraced balconies. Ziggurats; there are many of these stepped pyramids built for the worship of the Babylonian gods.
LANGUAGE	Aramaic is increasingly used throughout the Babylonian empire. You may be able to find help in learning this from the few Jews who travelled here before we were captured. Your children will pick it up naturally – make sure they are just as fluent in our Hebrew language!

What did the Babylonians do? If there had been a Job Centre in Babylon, the Jewish exiles might have seen notices like this:

· POSTS VACANT ·

FARMERS to grow a wide range of crops and tend varied animals.

SCHOLARS including some for a new project studying the movements of the planets.

SOLDIERS Must be ready for advanced training to Babylonian Army standards.

LAWYERS who will not be put off by the harsh punishments inflicted on criminals and traitors (thrown to lions, roasted alive over hot ashes etc...)

Psalm 137 describes how the Jews felt when they first arrived in Babylon.

They gradually became used to the different way of life in Babylon. Many, however, taught their children Jewish ways and beliefs, and looked forward to returning one day to their homeland in Palestine.

We'll never get used to all that!

I'll never forget life in Jerusalem!

They wanted us to sing them one of our Jewish songs – but how could we sing to the Lord in a foreign land?

Many people today are forced to move to other lands because of war or famine. Pray for these refugees, as they settle in strange places, and for those who try to help them.

ESTHER
THE BRAVE QUEEN

700 BC	600	500
/EXILE OF ISRAEL	/EXILE OF JUDAH	/ESTHER

The whole of the book of Esther is taken up with this exciting story from the time when the Jews were exiled in Babylon. The Persians had conquered Babylon, and made it part of their empire.

In the first two chapters of the book of Esther, we meet most of the characters of the story –

☐ King Xerxes, ruler of the Persian Empire, proud and wanting to show off his possessions.
☐ His Queen – Vashti – who dares disobey her husband!
☐ Mordecai, an exiled Jew living in the capital, Susa.
☐ Esther, Mordecai's beautiful niece.

King Xerxes organises a sort of 'Miss World' competition to find someone to replace Queen Vashti as his wife.

You can read for yourself in chapter 2 about the dramatic changes in Mordecai and Esther's lives as a result.

Chapter 3 introduces the villain, Haman, an ambitious, arrogant man appointed as prime minister. We find out about Haman's plot against Mordecai and the exiled Jews, and Esther's courageous efforts to save them. The story has a very interesting twist to it. You can find out for yourself in Esther chapter 7 who ends up hanging on Haman's unusually tall gallows!

But . . . where is God?
Although God is never mentioned once in the whole book of Esther, the story is an example of God's protection of the exiled Jews, and the importance of his timing in history. Here are some modern examples of people who, like Esther, were in a position to help, and obeyed – even though it was risky to do so:

Corrie ten Boom – a Dutch woman who hid many Jews and prevented them being taken to Hitler's gas chambers during the Second World War.

Janani Luwum – a former Archbishop of Uganda, who was murdered because he spoke out against the evil rule of General Amin.

David Wilkerson – a North American pastor who risked his life helping violent young drug addicts in New York from the late 1950s onwards.

Think of someone who is in an uncomfortable or dangerous place because they are serving God, and pray for them.

EZRA AND NEHEMIAH
GOING HOME

500 BC	450	400
/EZRA /NEHEMIAH		

The books of Ezra and Nehemiah tell about the return of the Jews from Assyria to their own land. Everything had to be rebuilt.

540 BC
First exiles return.

THE GOOD NEWS
Cyrus, King of Persia, conquers Babylon and says –

'THE JEWS CAN GO HOME, AND REBUILD THEIR TEMPLE – BUT STILL UNDER MY AUTHORITY.'

WHO WENT?
People from the tribes of Judah and Benjamin, led by Zerubbabel, and 'everyone else whose heart God had moved' (Ezra 1:5–6) – a long list!

HOW MANY?

SOMEONE WAS A CAREFUL ACCOUNTANT!

Exiles 42,360
Servants 7,337
Musicians 200
Horses 736
Mules 245
Camels 435
Donkeys 6,720
(Ezra 2:64–67)

THEY DID NOT GO EMPTY-HANDED!
They took silver utensils, gold, supplies, pack animals, other valuables and offerings for the temple plus the treasures that King Nebuchadnezzar had taken from Jerusalem (Ezra 1: 4–11).

Ezra Chapter 3 tells us that on arrival they:
- settled in their original towns around Jerusalem
- rebuilt the altar of the temple first – religious worship could now begin
- laid the foundation of the temple

BUT . . . not everyone is glad to see the Jews back.

Enemies stop work on temple for 15 years.

JEWS HALT!

JEWS STOP!

JEWS DON'T GO ON!

WHO ARE THESE PEOPLE?
They are people of mixed races and religions living around Jerusalem, and known as the Samaritans. Because of their mixed religion, they are not allowed to help rebuild the temple. So they bribe Persian officials to hold up the work, and cause trouble for many years. The full story is told in Ezra chapter 4, and Nehemiah chapters 4 and 6.

520 BC
The temple is completed.

Having given up building because of this opposition, the Jews only restart the building of the temple fifteen years later, when two prophets, Haggai and Zechariah, remind them –

YOU CAME HERE TO BUILD GOD'S HOUSE, NOT YOUR OWN.

The complete speech comes in the first chapter of Haggai. (Since Haggai and Zechariah were prophets, all their words to the Jews are printed in the Bible along with the other books of prophecy. See the books of Haggai and Zechariah.)

This challenge gets them going again, and the temple is finished, and 'joyfully dedicated' (Ezra 6:16).

No building done in Jerusalem for more than 60 years.

460 BC
Ezra returns with more Jews – city walls still broken down.

NEARLY 60 YEARS LATER

Another group of Jews, under the leadership of Ezra, a Jewish scholar and teacher, return to Jerusalem. Read Ezra chapters 8 and 9 for yourself, and find out what new problem faces Ezra on his return, and how he saves the Jews from the renewed danger of idolatry. The temple is completed, the Jews are re-organising themselves, but Jerusalem is not safe. Its broken down walls leave it open to enemy attacks. Who will organise the rebuilding of the city?

Back in Babylon one man is very upset when he hears the bad news from Jerusalem. Who is he?

445 BC
Nehemiah arrives, and work on walls completed in 52 days.

Nehemiah obtains permission from King Artaxerxes to go and help the Jews in Jerusalem rebuild the walls. After his arrival there, and his inspection of the walls, he plans his tactics.

TACTICS

Each clan responsible for their own section of the wall. Security guards and alarm system to protect the builders. Overtime! – work during the day, guard duty at night.

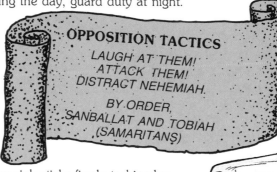

OPPOSITION TACTICS

LAUGH AT THEM!
ATTACK THEM!
DISTRACT NEHEMIAH.

BY ORDER,
SANBALLAT AND TOBIAH
(SAMARITANS)

Nehemiah sticks firmly to his plan, and their enemies fail to stop them. The wall – over a mile long – is built in 52 days; probably the fastest-built city wall in history!

PERSONAL DATA

Name – Nehemiah
Nationality – Exiled Jew
Occupation – wine steward to King Artaxerxes, the Persian king
Character reference – Man of prayer, faith and practical ability.

I WILL WORK WITH YOU.
GOD WILL HELP US DO IT.

SIGNED,
NEHEMIAH.

Nehemiah was a man of outstanding talents, but continually gave God the credit for everything that was done. Not only was the wall rebuilt, and Jerusalem made safe, but he and Ezra taught the Jews to obey God's laws, and organised their daily lives. Their leadership at this time of new beginnings prevented a return to idolatry. The nation now was reorganised, ready to go forward towards the climax of their history, when Jesus Christ was born four centuries later.

TODAY

Nehemiah was a man of prayer and action (for example, in Nehemiah 4:9, 'We prayed to our God, and kept men on guard against them day and night'.) God expects us to ask him for his help and then get down to work!

JOB
THE MAN WHO CHALLENGED GOD

Job is the first book of the so-called 'Wisdom Literature' (see also Proverbs, Ecclesiastes, some Psalms) about the sensible way to live.

FIRST ROUND, Job chapter 1.

MEET JOB
Wealthy and obedient to God.

SECOND ROUND, Job Chapter 2.

Penniless, bereaved and now covered in sores – Job *still* trusts God (Job 2: 7–10).

BUT – he wonders why all this has happened. In those days, people believed that riches were God's reward for being good, and trouble was a punishment for being bad. So – what had gone wrong?

Job's friends gathered round to tell him! (Job 3–37).

STOP! – it's God's turn now! (chap 38–41)

Job suddenly saw how great and caring God was – and how stupid he had been to question him! (Job 42: 1–6). God now healed and defended him right in front of his friends (Job 42: 7–16).

God's Last Word – 'Job's friends did not tell the truth about me. Job did, and even though he questioned me, he remained faithful.'

TODAY

The question of WHY people suffer is still not answered – perhaps because "Why?" is the wrong question to ask! God remains great and caring, whether things seem to go right or wrong – he is always in control.

For a modern 'Job-like' story, read 'Joni', the autobiography of Joni Eareckson, paralysed in an accident when she was seventeen.

PSALMS
SING A NEW SONG TO THE LORD

I FEEL AWFUL!

I'VE DONE TERRIBLE THINGS AGAINST YOU, GOD – I'M SORRY!

GOD, YOU'RE LIKE A BIG STRONG ROCK!

LET'S SHOUT AND SING – GOD IS SO GREAT!

I FEEL SO SMALL WHEN I THINK ABOUT HOW GREAT YOU ARE, GOD.

Perhaps you have felt or thought some of these things sometimes. The Jews did, and wrote songs about their thoughts and feelings. The Book of Psalms is a collection of them. Many were written by David; in some cases, no writer's name is given.

Some express the ups and downs in a *person's* life:

> I will always thank the Lord; I will never stop praising him! (Psalm 34:1)

Others express the ups and downs of the *nation's* life:

> 'Wake up Lord! Why are you asleep? Rouse yourself! Don't reject us for ever. (Psalm 44:23)

There are others where the writer is absorbed in thinking
- [ ] about God himself
- [ ] about what God has said
- [ ] or about some human problem.

How clearly the sky reveals God's glory! (Psalm 19:1)

The law of the Lord is perfect; it gives new strength. (Psalm 19:7)

Why do the wicked get away with it? (Psalm 73)

There are prophetic songs – Psalm 22 is the most well known – that give clues in advance about how Jesus will suffer while he is on earth . . .

My God, my God, why have you abandoned me? (v. 1)
All who see me jeer at me. (v. 7)
'You relied on the Lord,' they say – 'Why doesn't he save you?' (v. 8)
They tear at my hands and feet. (v. 16)
They gamble for my clothes. (v. 18)

. . . and how he will rule as a great king.

All nations will remember the Lord . . . From every part of the world they will turn to him . . . All races will worship him (v. 27)
All proud men will bow down to him. . . . All mortal men will bow down before him. (v. 29)

Now for some detective work.
Find the book of Matthew in your Bible (New Testament) and look up these verses – Matthew 27: 35, 39, 43, 46. Can you see the connection between them and Psalm 22? And look up Paul's letter to the Philippians, chapter 2 verses 8–11. Can you see the connection with Psalm 22 verses 27–29?

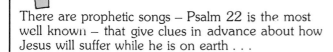

DAVID THE SONGWRITER

He wrote many of the Psalms. He thinks over past experience, present joys and sorrow, and turns them into song.

'The Lord is my shepherd... He lets me rest in fields of green grass, and leads me to quiet pools of fresh water. Your shepherd's rod and staff protect me.' (Psalm 23)

These words from the most famous Psalm of all are obviously based on David's experience as a shepherd.

David steals Bathsheba, another man's wife, and has her husband killed. Some time later, when Nathan the prophet helps him realise the wrong he has done, he is deeply sorry, and pours out his heart to God.

'Be merciful to me, O God, because of your constant love. I have sinned against you – only against you – and done what you consider evil... Create a pure heart in me, O God.' (Psalm 51)

David is not a dreamy poet – he is a strong warrior king, and many of the songs he wrote were thank you songs for God's help in battles against his enemies.

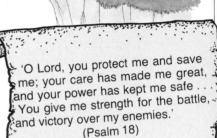

'O Lord, you protect me and save me; your care has made me great, and your power has kept me safe... You give me strength for the battle, and victory over my enemies.' (Psalm 18)

Great events were also recorded by David in song. This one was written to be sung in a triumphant march when the Covenant Box (symbol of God's presence) was brought into Jerusalem.

'Fling wide the gates, open the ancient doors, and the great king will come in... Who is this great king? He is the Lord, strong and mighty, the Lord, victorious in battle.' (Psalm 24)

TODAY

THIS SAYS IT FOR ME!

All of us feel a sense of wonder and relief when we discover someone else who thinks and feels the same way as we do. That is why people so enjoy reading the Psalms – 'I feel that too, but didn't know how to put it.' Look out for parts of Psalms that 'say it for you.'

MUSIC AND WORSHIP

WHY should we worship God?

Praise the Lord
Praise God in his temple
Praise his strength in heaven
Praise him for the mighty things he
has done
Praise him for his supreme
greatness.

HOW should we worship him?

Praise him with trumpets
Praise him with harps and lyres
Praise him with drums and dancing
Praise him with harps and flutes
Praise him with cymbals.

WHO should worship him?

Praise the Lord, all living creatures,
Praise the Lord (Psalm 150).

This Psalm (or hymn of praise) tells us that Jewish worship was lively and enthusiastic!

• Music was an important part of everyday life. They used INSTRUMENTS – wind, string, percussion.

• They used CHOIRS – sometimes of two groups responding to one another. 'Give thanks to the Lord because he is God.'
'His love is eternal' (Psalm 136).

• On big occasions (like the dedication of the walls of Jerusalem, Nehemiah chapter 12), choirs and orchestras joined together.

• A procession of singers and musicians marched round the rebuilt city walls. The singers sang at the top of their voices. Priests blowing trumpets marched next, followed by others, all of whom carried musical instruments. The noise they all made could be heard far and wide.

• Dancing was also used in worship. 'Praise him with drums and dancing' (Psalm 150). King David danced with all his might to honour the Lord when the ark was on its journey to Jerusalem (2 Samuel 6:14).

• Music was used not only to express joy, but sadness too, as in David's lament for Saul and Jonathan after their death (2 Samuel 1: 17–27). 'David sang this lament . . . and ordered it to be taught to the people of Judah.

• The whole of the Book of Lamentations is made up of sorrowful dirges about the destruction of Jerusalem. It is not certain whether these were used in worship, or just at times of national festivals of remembrance.

THE BOOKS OF WISDOM

PROVERBS

Proverbs, Job and Ecclesiastes are the books of 'wisdom literature' once used in the training of young men and especially those who would become national leaders. The writers include King Solomon, and they are full of useful comments on life, and helpful tips from their own experience.

AN IMPORTANT BEGINNING

There are often two ways of doing things – a right way . . . and a wrong way! Proverbs 1:7 says that the right way starts with God himself – 'To have knowledge (wisdom) you must first have reverence for the Lord.'

AFTER THAT

Here are some 'rights' to follow and some 'wrongs to avoid' –

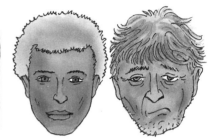

The Sensible Man . . .
- Will see trouble coming and avoid it
- Likes to be told when doing wrong
- Ignores an insult
- Works and will earn a living (assuming there's work for him)

. . . and his Sensible Wife
- Is her husband's pride and joy
- Is worth far more than jewels – find out how much more by reading this lovely poem in praise of her (Prov 31:10–31)

The Foolish Man . . .
- will walk right into it and regret it later (Prov 22:3)
- hates being corrected (Prov 12:1)
- shows his annoyance (Prov 12:16)
- sits around talking and remains poor (Prov 14:23)

. . . and his Foolish Wife
- brings shame on her husband, and is like cancer in his bones (Prov 12:4)
- her nagging is like water going drip-drip-drip (Prov 19: 13)

The writers touch on many topics:
- ☐ wealth and poverty
- ☐ family and friends
- ☐ hopes and fears
- ☐ words we speak
  and most important of all,
- ☐ our relationship with God.

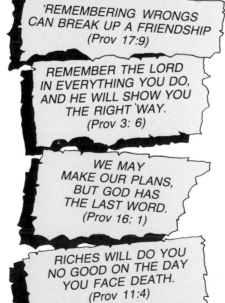

'REMEMBERING WRONGS CAN BREAK UP A FRIENDSHIP (Prov 17:9)

REMEMBER THE LORD IN EVERYTHING YOU DO, AND HE WILL SHOW YOU THE RIGHT WAY. (Prov 3: 6)

WE MAY MAKE OUR PLANS, BUT GOD HAS THE LAST WORD. (Prov 16: 1)

RICHES WILL DO YOU NO GOOD ON THE DAY YOU FACE DEATH. (Prov 11:4)

REVERENCE FOR THE LORD IS AN EDUCATION IN ITSELF! (Prov 15:33)

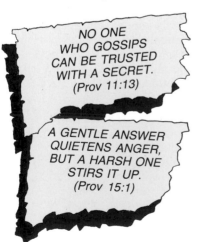

NO ONE WHO GOSSIPS CAN BE TRUSTED WITH A SECRET. (Prov 11:13)

A GENTLE ANSWER QUIETENS ANGER, BUT A HARSH ONE STIRS IT UP. (Prov 15:1)

TODAY

Today's world is very different from Solomon's, but people have not changed, and these tips for life are as important for the 20th century as for 1,000 BC! Some are easier to put into practice than others.

BOOKS OF POETRY AND WISDOM

ECCLESIASTES

Not a book to read when we are feeling depressed!
It reflects the emptiness of life without God.

WHO WROTE IT?

A poor man who had a tough life? No! The writer
sees things from the point of view of someone who
had everything this world could offer.

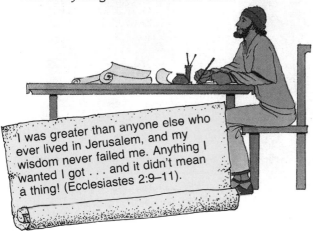

'I was greater than anyone else who ever lived in Jerusalem, and my wisdom never failed me. Anything I wanted I got . . . and it didn't mean a thing! (Ecclesiastes 2:9–11).

WHAT DID HE DECIDE IN THE END?

That if you look at life just in this world – as if there's
nothing beyond it – nothing has any meaning.

'Everything leads to weariness – a weariness too great for words' (Eccl 1:8).

WHY DID HE WRITE IT?

'The philosopher tried to find comforting words, but
the words he wrote were honest' (Eccl 12:10). He
wanted people to face reality. Not that we'd always
understand *why* things happen, but so we'd know
what to do about them.

HOW CAN I MAKE THE BEST USE OF THE HOLIDAY, EVEN THOUGH I'M ILL?

WHY DO I HAVE TO BE ILL JUST AT HOLIDAY TIME?

Which is the most useful (wise) question to ask?
BUT on the other hand, if you take account of God,
then everything has meaning.

'God is going to judge everything we do, whether good or bad, even things done in secret' (Eccl 12:14).

If it matters that much to him, then it should matter
to us.

SONG OF SONGS

This is a collection of love poems. What do they
say? – Love is great!

The fact that this is in the Bible shows that the
physical expression of love between man and

HOW BEAUTIFUL YOU ARE, MY LOVE. (Song of Songs 1:15)

HOW HANDSOME YOU ARE, MY DEAREST. (Song of Songs 1:16)

woman – within God's laws – is beautiful and good;
not something to be embarrassed or ashamed of.

The Bible sometimes uses such human love as a
picture of God's love for his people.

Therefore some Christians have understood the
Song of Solomon in this way also – as a poetic
description of the love between the Lord Jesus Christ
and his 'bride' the church (all who belong to him
by faith). Read Ephesians 5:25 and Revelation
19:7–8 to see how the New Testament puts this.

GOD SPEAKS THROUGH PROPHETS

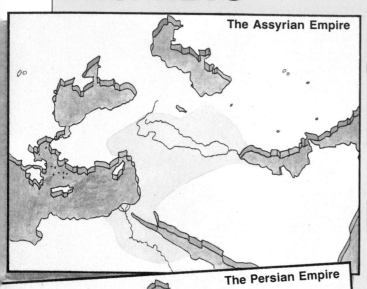

The Assyrian Empire

The Persian Empire

The Babylonian Empire

WHAT IS A PROPHET?

A PROPHET IS SOMEONE WHO TELLS PEOPLE WHAT GOD WANTS THEM TO KNOW.

OH YES. WE HAVE ALREADY MET ELIJAH AND ELISHA, HAVEN'T WE? THEY WERE IN THE BOOKS OF KINGS.

STORIES ABOUT ELIJAH AND ELISHA WERE WRITTEN DOWN BY THE WRITERS OF THE BOOKS OF KINGS. THEY RECORDED MANY OTHER THINGS TOO. THE BOOKS WE ARE GOING TO LOOK AT NOW GIVE THE MESSAGE OF ONE PROPHET.

THE MESSAGE?

YES. THE PROPHETS WE ARE GOING TO LEARN ABOUT SPOKE TO THE PEOPLE AND RULERS OF THE TIME. IT WAS A TIME OF GREAT DIFFICULTY FOR ISRAEL. THE PEOPLE WERE BEING THREATENED BY FOREIGN POWERS. THEY ASSUMED THAT GOD WOULD PROTECT THEM BUT THEY WERE NEGLECTING TO WORSHIP HIM OR KEEP HIS COMMANDMENTS. MANY PEOPLE WERE WORSHIPPING OTHER GODS.

TELL ME WHAT THE PROPHETS SAID.

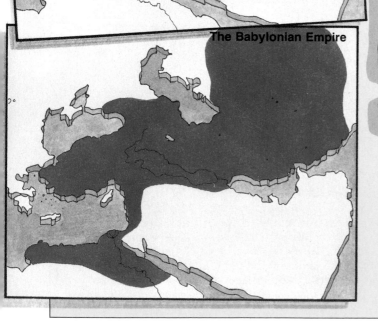

WELL, THEIR MESSAGES WERE OFTEN TO DO WITH GREAT EVENTS THAT WERE HAPPENING AT THE TIME. LOOK AT THESE MAPS. THEY SHOW HOW THE EMPIRES OF MESOPOTAMIA GREW UP. EACH ONE BECAME MORE POWERFUL THAN THE LAST.

TROUBLE AHEAD FOR ISRAEL! THEY ARE ABOUT TO BE SWALLOWED UP!

THAT IS EXACTLY WHAT HAPPENED IN THE END.

WHY DIDN'T GOD PROTECT HIS PEOPLE?

THAT'S JUST IT. MOST PEOPLE ASSUMED HE WOULD!

I REMEMBER. GOD MADE THEM A PROMISE MANY YEARS AGO IN MOSES' TIME. IF THEY OBEYED HIM HE WOULD PROTECT THEM.

EXACTLY! BUT THE PEOPLE WERE NOT KEEPING THEIR SIDE OF THE BARGAIN. THEY WORSHIPPED OTHER GODS, ILL-TREATED THE POOR AND DIDN'T CARE ABOUT WHAT WAS HAPPENING IN THE POWERFUL NATIONS AROUND THEM. THEY IGNORED THE WARNINGS OF GOD'S PROPHETS AND SO IN TIME THEY WERE. . . .

SWALLOWED UP!

LOOK AT THIS CHART. IT SHOWS ROUGHLY WHEN EACH OF THE PROPHETS LIVED AND WHAT WAS GOING ON IN THOSE TIMES.

800 BC   ● Amos   ?Joel

● Jonah

● Hosea

● Micah   ● Isaiah

Northern kingdom, Israel, invaded. People exiled to Assyria 722

700

● Nahum

● Zephaniah

Jeremiah ●   ● Habbakuk

● Daniel

600

Southern kingdom, Judah, invaded. People exiled to Babylon 597

● Ezekiel

● Obadiah

Conquest of Babylonia by Persian king, Cyrus II. Exiled Jews sent home. Jerusalem and temple rebuilt 539

● Haggai   ● Zechariah

500

● Malachi

Prophets and main events

400

57

AMOS, HOSEA, ISAIAH, JONAH, JOEL, MICAH, JEREMIAH
BEFORE THE EXILE

AMOS

Amos was a shepherd who preached in the northern kingdom about the middle of the eighth century BC.

> 'The people of Israel have sinned again and again, and for this I will certainly punish them. They sell into slavery honest men who cannot pay their debts, poor men who cannot repay even the price of a pair of sandals. They trample down the weak and helpless and push the poor out of the way.' Amos 2:6,7.

God was angry with his people because their worship of him was not sincere. How could it be when they treated the poor so cruelly? God tells them:

> 'I hate your religious festivals. I cannot stand them! When you bring me burnt offerings and grain offerings I will not accept them . . . Stop your noisy songs. I do not want to listen to your harps. Instead let justice flow like a river that never goes dry.' Amos 5:21–24.

Amos had visions from God of the punishments he would send. Locusts would eat all the crops; fire would destroy the land. Amos begged God to relent and he did. But the people did not change. Amos had another vision. God was standing beside a wall, holding a plumbline (a weighted line used to check that the wall is straight).

AMOS, WHAT DO YOU SEE?

A PLUMBLINE

I AM USING IT TO SHOW THAT MY PEOPLE ARE LIKE A WALL THAT IS OUT OF LINE. I WILL NOT CHANGE MY MIND ABOUT PUNISHING THEM.

Amos 7:7,8.

Yet Amos finished his message on a note of hope. He looked forward to a time, after the punishment, when God promised: 'I will plant my people on the land I gave them and they will not be pulled up again' Amos 11:15.

A MESSAGE FOR TODAY
Read Amos 8:4–6 and Hosea 7:1. Both these men were deeply concerned about the treatment of the poor by the rich. Our world is like that today. The West is rich. Two thirds of the world do not have enough to eat. We have a responsibility to share our wealth with poorer countries.

HOSEA

Hosea also preached in the northern kingdom. He lived just after Amos.

Hosea had some sad things happen to him in his life. His wife ran away and became a prostitute. Eventually she became a slave. Hosea went after her and brought her back. All this heartbreak helped him to see how God must feel about Israel, who was behaving just like his wife. Just as she thought other men would take better care of her than her husband, so Israel followed foreign gods, thanking them for the harvests God had given them.

'She would never acknowledge that I am the one who gave her the corn, the wine, the olive oil and all the silver and gold she used in the worship of Baal, so at harvest time I will take back my gifts of corn and wine, and I will take away the wool and linen I gave her for clothes. . . . I will turn her vineyards and orchards into a wilderness; wild animals will destroy them. I will punish her for the times that she forgot me and burnt incense to Baal.' Hosea 2:8,9,12,13.

'They ask for revelations from a piece of wood! A stick tells them what to do!' Hosea 4:12.

God was very angry but he also had great love for them. Read Hosea 2:14–23. Here is a small part.

'Israel, I will make you my wife: I will be true and faithful: I will show you constant love and mercy and make you mine for ever.'

and in chapter eleven he says:

'. . . I was the one who taught Israel to walk. I took my people up in my arms, but they did not acknowledge that I took care of them. I drew them to me with affection and love. I picked them up and held them to my cheek; I bent down and fed them.' Hos 11:3,4.

He knows that they will only learn with time and that he must allow them to be conquered.

'They refuse to return home, and so they must return to Egypt and Assyria will rule them . . . How can I give you up, Israel? How can I abandon you?' Hos 11:8.

But, like Amos, Hosea looks forward to a new future for Israel afterwards. 'I will be to the people of Israel like rain in a dry land. They will blossom like flowers' (Hos 14:5).

ISAIAH

Written by a nobleman living in Jerusalem in the last half of the eighth century BC.

The most famous parts are the 'servant songs', which Christians believe are about the coming Messiah. Isaiah also wrote about the need to live as God wants and the future importance of Jerusalem in the world.

'Don't think that the Lord is too weak to save you or too deaf to hear you call for help. It is because of your sins that he doesn't hear you.' Chapter 59:1,2.

'Arise, Jerusalem, and shine like the sun. The glory of the Lord is shining on you!' Chapter 60:1.

The Assyrians had invaded the northern kingdom, Israel. The King of Israel now had to do as the Assyrians said.

Isaiah's message: A warning that this will happen to Judah too.

'It seemed to me that Israel was like a vineyard that the Lord had planted and cared for lovingly. When the harvest came every grape was sour' (chapter 5:2). 'I was sad. One day I saw a great vision of the Lord in all his majesty and glory filling our great temple. He asked for a messenger to go to the people. I said "I will go. Send me" ' (chapter 6).

'I told the people that the Emperor of Assyria would come to attack them' (Isaiah 8:7). 'Of course they would not listen and God had told me that this would happen. I told them that the people who walked in darkness would one day see a great light – a ruler who would rule as a successor of King David with power, right and justice until the end of time' (Isaiah 9:2–7).

'After God had allowed Assyria to punish the people he would punish Assyria in turn and the people who were exiled would return' (Chapter 10–11).

CHAPTERS 40–66 These chapters look forward to the ending of the exile and the return to Israel.

'Do not be afraid. I will save you. I have called you by name. You are mine.' Chapter 43:1–2.

'From the distant east and the far west I will bring your people home.' Chapter 43:5.

JONAH

The story of a man sent by God to preach to the people of Nineveh, the capital of Assyria. He refused and ran away. The ship on which he was travelling met a great storm. The sailors, thinking he was to blame, threw him overboard. He was swallowed by a great fish which vomited him up on the shores of Nineveh. This time he did as God asked!

JOEL

Describes a terrible plague of locusts and a drought. Joel saw this as a picture of what would happen to Israel if she did not turn back to God. 'The day of the Lord is coming soon. It will be a dark and gloomy day . . . The great army of locusts advances like darkness spreading over the mountains' (Joel 2:1–2). But . . . 'I will pour out my spirit on everyone (Joel. 2:28). 'I will restore the prosperity of Judah and Jerusalem. Then, Israel, you will know that I am the Lord your God' (Joel 3:1,17).

MICAH

Southern kingdom.
Worked during the years before Assyria invaded Judah.

HEY! DON'T FORGET ME! I LIVED AT THE SAME TIME AS ISAIAH. I TRIED TO WARN EVERYONE OF WHAT WAS GOING TO HAPPEN. THE ASSYRIANS HAD GOT SAMARIA. JERUSALEM WAS NEXT! I KNEW THAT IN THE END JUDAH'S ENEMIES WOULD CRAWL IN THE DUST LIKE SNAKES (Micah 7:14–17). BUT FIRST JUDAH WOULD SUFFER. HOW I WISHED THEY HAD LISTENED.

A MESSAGE FOR TODAY

All this took place because the people disobeyed God, oppressed the weak and ignored those who needed help. How about us? We should think about what is happening on our planet today and of the consequences.

NUCLEAR WEAPONS.
POLLUTION.
STARVATION.
WAR.

These things too can be avoided if we live according to God's values rather than our own.

JEREMIAH

I lived just before and during the final disaster when Jerusalem was destroyed and everyone was carried off to Babylon. This was in 586 BC. No one listened to me either. How I suffered!
People tried to kill me. I complained to God, 'Everyone

'The pain. I can't bear the pain! My heart! My heart is beating wildly. I can't keep quiet. I hear the trumpets and the shouts of battle' (Jeremiah 4: 19).

jeers at me. They mock me all day long. Why was I born? Was it only to have trouble and sorrow, to end my life in disgrace?'
I did all kinds of things to make the people listen. I even walked about with an ox yoke on my neck to show the people that they would be slaves (Jeremiah 27).

I read the king my message. He took each bit as I finished, cut it with his knife and threw it on the fire. I had to write it all out again.
Finally when I just wouldn't stop they threw me down a pit and left me there. Nebuchadnezzar came and destroyed the city and the temple and took the people away to Babylon. He was the only one who thought what I had said was sensible. He set me free. I was able to begin working again. I told the exiles to settle down, to build and to plant and marry and be prepared for a long stay. One day the Babylonian empire would be destroyed and they would return.

LAMENTATIONS

The book of Lamentations was written after the destruction of Jerusalem. To lament means to cry out or complain about something. These poems mourn the ruin of the Temple and the city and ask God to bring the people back from exile.

NAHUM, ZEPHANIAH, HABBAKUK, OBADIAH, DANIEL, EZEKIEL

IN EXILE

650 BC	600	550

ISRAEL & JUDAH IN EXILE

BUT DID IT WORK THEN, THIS PUNISHMENT OR EXILE?

IT CERTAINLY DID! AT FIRST THE PEOPLE THOUGHT GOD HAD DESERTED THEM. SOME THOUGHT HE WAS NOT AS POWERFUL AS THE BABYLONIAN GODS. SOME THOUGHT HE WAS LEFT BEHIND IN ISRAEL. 'HOW CAN WE WORSHIP GOD IN A FOREIGN LAND?'

they asked in Psalm 137.

As time passed the people realised that God was not weak or absent, and that what had happened was no accident. It had happened to show them something: GOD WAS THE ONLY GOD OF THE WHOLE WORLD. This idea led to a wonderful new way of worshipping God as the people became determined not to make the same mistakes again.
☐ They made gathering places where they could meet for worship and to study God's word – SYNAGOGUES.
☐ They needed teachers to teach them the scriptures – RABBIS.
☐ God led them to collect together the stories and traditions to form a written text – THE HEBREW BIBLE.
☐ They decided to remember God properly in their daily lives so they practised CIRCUMCISION and KEPT THE SABBATH AND FESTIVALS.

These two prophets spoke just before the exile.

NAHUM

The three chapters of this book are a poem celebrating the destruction of Nineveh in 612 BC.

ZEPHANIAH

lived at the same time as Jeremiah. He prophesied the destruction of Jerusalem. 'I will punish the people of Jerusalem and all Judah. I will destroy the last traces of the worship of Baal.' He spoke of the destruction of Assyria (Zephaniah 1: 4). His book ends, 'Rejoice with all your heart, Jerusalem . . . I will bring your scattered people home.' (Zephaniah 3:14,20).

These two prophets spoke during the exile.

HABBAKUK

This is a tiny book in which the prophet complains to God about the violence of the Babylonians. God explains that it is all part of his purpose.

OBADIAH

This book has only one chapter. Edom, Judah's enemy, had rejoiced over her capture. Obadiah foretells that Edom, and in fact all Israel's enemies, will be destroyed.

DANIEL

The book of Daniel is set in the reign of Nebuchadnezzar, King of Babylon. Here are some of the most famous stories about Daniel and his friends.

1 Daniel asks that he and his friends be allowed to eat vegetables (chapter 1). Babylonian food was forbidden to Jews (Deuteronomy 14:3–21).

2 Daniel interprets the king's dream. It means that none of the world empires will survive (chapter 2).

3 Daniel's three friends refuse to worship a golden statue. They are put into a fiery furnace but are unharmed (chapter 3).

4 Daniel explains another dream to the king which predicts that he will be mad for a while (chapter 4).

5 Belshazzar holds a feast during which writing appears on the wall. Daniel explains its meaning (chapter 5).

6 Daniel is imprisoned in a den of lions for worshipping God (chapter 6).

The rest of the book contains many visions that Daniel had. They showed that the great empires that would arise after the Babylonians would not survive.

A MESSAGE FOR TODAY

God never abandons his people although they may have to endure suffering. Some people today have been exiled because of their religious beliefs.

The Russian poetess Irina Ratushinskaya who is living in exile in the West.

EZEKIEL

I was living in Babylon at the time when Jerusalem was destroyed. I saw a wonderful vision of the Lord. He gave me a scroll to eat, which tasted sweet as honey. This showed me that from then on it was my job to speak for God to the people of Israel (chapters 1–3). The Lord told me to act out the siege of Jerusalem (chapters 4–5). But there was also hope. One day I found myself standing in a valley that was full of dry bones. . . .

> MORTAL MAN, CAN THESE BONES COME BACK TO LIFE?

> SOVEREIGN LORD, ONLY YOU CAN ANSWER THAT!

> PROPHESY TO THE BONES! TELL THESE DRY BONES TO LISTEN TO THE WORD OF THE LORD . . . I AM GOING TO PUT BREATH INTO YOU AND BRING YOU BACK TO LIFE.

Next God told me to take two sticks, one named Judah and one named Israel. I was to hold them together end to end as one stick. This was how he showed me that one day the two kingdoms would join together as one people again.

A MESSAGE FOR TODAY

On these two pages we learn about Israel's relations with foreigners. They were not always friendly. Jonah did not want God to show mercy to Israel's enemy, Assyria. He had to learn the hard way what God wanted. God still wants us to tell people of all nations about his love for them.

Before my very eyes there was a great rattling and the bones joined together and breath entered their bodies. I knew then that the dead bones of Israel would live again (chapter 37:1–4).

> WHICH PROPHETS ARE LEFT NOW?

> WELL, THERE ARE THE PROPHETS WHO RETURNED HOME WITH THE PEOPLE AFTER THE EXILE.

AFTER THE EXILE

550 BC	500	450

/RETURN FROM EXILE

HAGGAI

Spoke in 520 BC. The people had been back in their homeland for some time but the temple had not been rebuilt. Haggai explains that this is why the harvests have been poor.

ZECHARIAH

Had visions from 518–520 BC. He too was concerned with the rebuilding of the temple and future prosperity for Israel. For Christians his most famous passage is Zechariah 9:9, where he speaks of a future king humble and riding on a donkey. See Matthew 21:1–9.

AND FINALLY

MALACHI

Writes after the rebuilding of the temple. He is worried that the priests are not doing their job properly. They are offering worthless gifts to God. He reminds all the people that they should not cheat God. If they give generously to God he will bless them.

'I will not let insects destroy your crops, and your grapevines will be loaded with grapes' (Malachi 3:11). Locusts are still a plague to farmers in many parts of the world, as they were in Bible times.

ALEXANDER TO THE ROMANS

This is the period of history not covered by the books of the Bible.

The Greek amphitheatre at Philippi.

A coin bearing the head of Antiochus.

330 BC

Alexander the Great conquered the Persians. Israel had been part of the Persian Empire so now it belonged to the Greeks. There was much about Greek life and thought that attracted the Jews. Some, even priests, began to be influenced by their ways. Others thought everything Greek must be avoided because the Greeks worshipped idols.

170–165 BC

From 170–165 BC Antiochus Epiphanes, a descendant of one of Alexander's generals, ruled Israel. He aimed to wipe out the Jewish religion. He set up a statue of the Greek god Zeus in the temple. His soldiers forced Jews in every village to sacrifice a pig (to a Jew an unclean animal) to the Greek gods. At one village a priest and his five sons rebelled. Under the leadership of one son, Judas Maccabeus (The Hammerer), the Jews won several battles and the temple was rededicated. The family ruled Israel as the Hasmoneans until family quarrels led the Romans to intervene in 63 BC.

TIME OF JESUS

THE JEWS UNDER THE ROMANS

The Romans knew how to handle the rebellious Jews. They brought thousands of soldiers into this tiny land. As Jewish men would not fight on the Sabbath they could not be used for Roman armies. Instead very heavy taxes were demanded. The Romans also expected them to worship the Emperor but the Jews worshipped God alone. They longed for the Messiah, God's anointed one, promised in Isaiah and other books. The reign of Herod the Great made them desperate. Although he built a magnificent temple for the Jews they hated him for his friendship with the Romans. Jesus was born during his reign. Finally in AD 66 the Jews began a war with Rome and lost. In AD 70 the temple was destroyed. A group of 1,000 Zealots hid in Herod's rock fortress Masada. After a long siege they committed suicide rather than surrender to the Romans.

MASADA
AD 73

GREAT NEWS
A LOOK AT THE GOSPELS

READ ALL ABOUT IT!

There's certainly no shortage of news these days. The average daily newspaper finds enough news to cover more than thirty pages every day. And there is probably plenty more news which they choose not to print.

Unfortunately most of the news is *bad* news. It always has been. Sadly many people find bad news more exciting than good news.

But that's what made the early Christians so different. They knew that they had good news, so good that they wanted to share it with the whole world. That good news was about Jesus, the son of God, who had come to bring new life to mankind.

At first this good news was shared by word of mouth. Preachers, evangelists, missionaries and teachers talked to all who would listen. But then as those who had known Jesus grew older, it became clear that the good news had to be written down.

And so over a period of around thirty years, towards the end of the first century AD, the good news about the life, death and resurrection of Jesus was written down.

THE WRITERS

The writers of the four gospels were not professional journalists. They were, however, four men who were led by God to write what they knew to be true.

☐ **Matthew** – an ex-tax collector for the Roman government.
☐ **Mark** – John Mark is his full name. He later went with Paul and Barnabas on their missionary travels.
☐ **Luke** – a doctor who gave up medicine for travelling with Paul and writing. He wrote the Acts too.
☐ **John** – once a fisherman and one of Jesus' disciples. Later a church leader and a writer of several other New Testament books.

THE READERS

The four accounts of the good news were written for different readers who lived in different cities. Their needs were also different. And so each of the gospels, although sharing the same good news, is not an exact reprint of the others.

● **Matthew** – probably written for Jewish readers
● **Mark** – probably written for readers in Rome
● **Luke** – probably written for Gentile (non-Jewish) readers
● **John** – probably written for Christians in Asia Minor (Turkey)

MATTHEW
MEET THE KING

| 0 | AD 20 | 40 |

/BIRTH OF JESUS

/JESUS' DEATH, RESURRECTION, ASCENSION

WHERE IS THE ONE WHO HAS BEEN BORN KING OF THE JEWS?

The King of the Jews is born just as the prophets said – chapters 1 & 2.

BLESSED IS HE WHO COMES IN THE NAME OF THE LORD.

The King comes to the capital and to his enemies – chapters 19–25.

YOU ARE THE CHRIST.

The King is recognised and teaches again about his kingdom – chapters 16–18.

PREPARE THE WAY FOR THE LORD.

The way for the King is prepared by John the Baptist. Jesus prepares himself – chapters 3 & 4.

JESUS, KING OF THE JEWS

Rejected and killed – chapters 26–27.

NOT EVERYONE . . . WILL ENTER THE KINGDOM . . . ONLY HE WHO DOES THE WILL OF MY FATHER.

How to live in the kingdom – chapters 5–7.

HE HAS RISEN!

chapter 28:6

THE KINGDOM OF HEAVEN IS LIKE TREASURE HIDDEN IN A FIELD.

Jesus teaches about his kingdom – chapters 13–15.

WHAT KIND OF MAN IS THIS? EVEN THE WINDS AND WAVES OBEY HIM.

The King shows his power over disease, nature and men – chapters 8 & 9.

GO AND MAKE DISCIPLES OF ALL NATIONS.

chapter 28:19.

FOR THE SON OF MAN IS LORD OF THE SABBATH.

The King makes claims about himself and for himself – chapters 10–12.

MATTHEW

THE MAN PEOPLE LOVED TO HATE . . .

Matthew certainly wasn't everybody's idea of a best friend. When it came to the top of the popularity list, Matthew was nowhere to be seen in the Top Ten.

Most people avoided him, despised him and left him right out of their lives. Matthew was a collector of taxes. And when you had said that, for most people, you had said enough!

. . . BECAME THE MAN JESUS LOVED TO HAVE AS A FRIEND

And that made many people look surprised as the two of them walked along the street together. That a good man like Jesus should want a bad man like Matthew for a friend was beyond their understanding.

But to Jesus it all made sense. 'After all,' said Jesus to those who criticised him for choosing Matthew for his friend, 'it would be a poor doctor who spent so much time with healthy patients that he had no time for those who were really ill.' Jesus came to care for those who were spiritually sick.

And Matthew was one of those on the sick list.

'TRAITOR. FANCY WORKING FOR THE ROMANS!'

'YOU OUGHT TO BE FIGHTING AGAINST THEM NOT WORKING FOR THEM.'

'YOU'RE A THIEF. YOU TAKE MORE THAN YOU SHOULD AND THEN POCKET THE EXTRA FOR YOURSELF.'

Matthew was thrilled to discover that Jesus cared for him and that God would forgive him for all the wrong in his past life. He wanted his friends to hear the good news too. And so he threw a party. 'Come and have a party,' he said. 'There will be food and drink and music. But most of all Jesus will be there. Come and meet him.'

Jesus wants us to share the good news about him with our friends too.

RULERS OF THE WORLD
THE POWER OF THE ROMAN ARMY

MEET THE EMPIRE

Rome was the Super Power of New Testament times. Once just a group of peasant settlements beside the River Tiber, Rome was now the most powerful nation in the world. Her empire stretched from Spain to Palestine with all the lands in between these two countries under Rome's control.

The Romans were proud of their empire and enjoyed the wealth that trade brought them. For those whose lands were conquered, Rome brought law and order, though at a cost. Conquered nations had to pay high taxes and Roman rule was often harsh.

MEET THE ARMY

Countries conquered by the Roman armies became provinces of the Empire. Peace was maintained by garrisons of Roman soldiers. In Palestine there were probably about 120 Roman horsemen stationed and between 2,500 and 5,000 foot soldiers. Each soldier would be a member of a *century* – a group of about 100 soldiers. They were under the command of a *centurion*.

Matthew tells a story about a centurion who begged Jesus to heal his sick servant. Jesus was surprised at the man's faith (Matthew 8: 5–13). In Acts 10 we read how a Roman centurion, Cornelius, became a Christian.

MEET THE RULERS

Augustus Caesar was the Roman Emperor at the time of Jesus' birth. It was at his command that Joseph and Mary travelled to Bethlehem for the census (Luke 2:1). His boast was that he had found Rome brick and had left it marble. Certainly he was a strong ruler. His reforms covered political and military life in Rome. He also did much to revive religion and rebuilt many temples. In some places he was even worshipped as 'Dominus et Deus' (Lord and God).

Pontius Pilate was the man 'in charge' of Palestine. He lived at Caesarea. On special days, however, when there was a risk of trouble, he took his troops and moved to Jerusalem.

As governor or *procurator* of the province Pilate had full control. He alone could sentence a man to death. And that, of course, was why the Jewish religious leaders took Jesus to be tried before him. (See John 18:28–19:16).

MATTHEW

THE JESUS LIFESTYLE

Jesus spent a lot of his time on earth talking to ordinary people about how to live.

Matthew tells us about one day when Jesus sat on a hillside talking to crowds of people. What he said is known as 'The Sermon on the Mount'. You can find it in chapters 5–7.

In the first part of the sermon he shows that God values qualities in people that most people consider to be worthless. Jesus turned the world's values upside down.

WHAT MAKES A HAPPY AND SUCCESSFUL PERSON?

The traditional site of the Sermon on the Mount.

THE WORLD SAYS
1. Think big! Sell yourself.
2. Use others to get what you want.
3. Be one of the gang. Anything goes if it helps you to get on.
4. Look after yourself; never mind others.
5. Don't be afraid to stir up trouble.
6. Happiness is doing what *you* want to do.

JESUS SAYS
1. Don't rely on yourself. Ask God to help you. (Matt. 5:3,5)
2. Love your enemies. (Matt. 5:43)
3. Be glad when people insult you because you are my followers. (Matt. 5:11,12)
4. Be kind to others. (Matt. 5:7)
5. Work for peace. (Matt. 5:9)
6. If you want to be happy, do what God wants. (Matt. 5:6)

That's the way to *real* happiness, said Jesus.

Jesus used picture language to describe how a Christian is meant to be different.

YOU SHOULD BE   **YOU SHOULD NOT BE**

Like salt which brings out the flavour in food

Like salt with the flavour washed out by the rain – good for nothing.

Like light which leads through darkness

Like a torch without a battery. No good to anyone in the dark.

YOU AND YOUR RELIGION

You're right, said Jesus. Religion does make a difference to the way you treat others and the way you treat God.

But you're wrong when you go to church, pray, or give money to the poor only to make others think how good you are.

YOU AND YOUR ATTITUDE

The trouble is, said Jesus, you look at other people's faults but don't see your own. It's like trying to take a speck of dust out of someone's eye, when there's a log in your own eye!

Jesus said that anyone who lives his way is like a wise man who built his house on rock – hard work, but worthwhile when the storms come!

But anyone who does not listen to what Jesus says is like a silly man who built his house on sand – easy, but what a disaster when the storms come!

YOU AND GOD'S LAW

The Ten Commandments, said Jesus, are here to stay and to be obeyed. And it's no good feeling smug. I can hear your mind at work. You may not have murdered anyone, but have you never been unjustly angry with somebody and called him stupid? That is just as bad in God's eyes.

YOU AND YOUR LIFE

Are you sure that you have got your values right? Just look at you, said Jesus. You spend hours working, saving and buying things. Things that can be here today and gone tomorrow. It's all quite ridiculous really. A moth can destroy your clothes and a burglar steal your valuables.

And then you worry about clothes and food when one look around you at the birds and flowers should teach you to trust God for these things as long as you are doing what he wants.

CHANCE OF A LIFETIME

WANTED!

Twelve men to be in at the start of something great. No pay promised! No holidays! No comforts.

Successful applicants must be prepared to be away from home for long periods, to travel, to be hated, and misunderstood and to be ready for the unexpected. The work is dangerous and could result in death. No time wasters, please, who are looking for quick results and easy money.

If Jesus had wanted to advertise to find suitable men to be his twelve disciples, that is what he might have said.

Here are some of the people who thought they might become Jesus' disciples.

THE CURIOUS

Some came to find out more about the job but soon left when they discovered what the job really involved. (See John 6:60).

THE KEEN BUT CLUELESS

Some got really excited at the thought of working with Jesus. But when Jesus explained to them what would be expected of them, they had second thoughts and left. (See Luke 9:57–62).

THE COOL HEADED

Others understood clearly the demands which Jesus was making. They accepted the challenge. And when Jesus offered them the job, they agreed gladly. (See Mark 1:14–20).

THE MEN JESUS CHOSE

It's a bit of a surprise to discover the men Jesus chose for his disciples.

PETER

A tough fisherman, known as Simon to his family. He came from Galilee and his strong northern accent gave him away down south in Jerusalem (Mark 14:70).

His brother, Andrew, introduced him to Jesus. One day by the lakeside, Jesus called him to leave his fishing nets and follow him. Jesus gave him the name Peter, meaning 'a rock'. Peter became one of the three disciples closest to Jesus and was the first to declare openly, 'You are the Messiah' (Mark 8:27–30).

He was warm-hearted and eager and not afraid to speak out. But when Jesus was arrested, Peter was afraid and denied that he was a follower of Jesus. Afterwards he was very ashamed. Jesus forgave him and told him he still had work for him to do. (John 21:15–19) After Jesus went back to heaven, Peter was a leader of the Christian church at Jerusalem. The Jewish leaders put him in prison for preaching about Jesus but God let him out! (Acts 5:19, Acts 12:6–10). Later he travelled widely, preaching the good news, and wrote two of the New Testament letters (1 Peter and 2 Peter) to encourage new Christians. No one is certain about his death but he probably died during the persecution of Christians by the Roman Emperor Nero.

JUDAS

- A man with an eye for money.
- Was treasurer for the twelve and sometimes helped himself from the money bag (John 12:4–6).
- Turned against Jesus and betrayed him to the Jewish leaders for thirty silver coins (Matthew 26:14–16).
- Changed his mind and took the money back when he heard Jesus was condemned (Matthew 27:3–5).
- Hanged himself.

JAMES AND JOHN

Brothers who were fishermen. Jesus gave them the nickname 'sons of thunder' for their quick temper. They were Jesus' closest friends, along with Peter. The other ten disciples were angry because one day James and John asked Jesus for a special place in his kingdom. Jesus did not agree to their selfish request. He said they would have to suffer like him (Mark 10:35–41). Later, James was killed by King Herod. After Jesus' ascension, John, with Peter, preached fearlessly about Jesus, in spite of threats against them (Acts 4:18–20). He wrote the gospel of John, three New Testament letters and the book of Revelation.

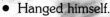

Jesus made it clear what he expects of those who want to follow him:

'If anyone wants to come with me he must forget self, carry his cross, and follow me. For whoever wants to save his own life will lose it; but whoever loses his life for me and for the gospel will save it.' (Mark 8:34–36).

'If a person is ashamed of me and of my teaching . . . then the Son of Man will be ashamed of him when he comes in the glory of his Father with the holy angels.' (Mark 8:38).

MARK
MEET GOD'S SERVANT

To be a Christian in first century Rome was to live dangerously. The Emperor Nero made sure of that. Under his orders Christians were arrested, often given an unfair trial and then killed – some were thrown to the lions or burned alive.

Those who managed to escape arrest took refuge in the tunnels beneath the city of Rome. Here Christians set up home and also met for worship. They were literally an underground church.

Despite the persecution many others joined the Christians. The new members were anxious to learn as much as possible about their new faith. There was always great excitement when someone like Peter visited the Christians. He had been a disciple of Jesus.

But there was always the possibility that Peter might be killed. He had already been in prison several times for his faith. How would new converts to the Christian faith learn about Jesus if that happened? It became clear that the good news about Jesus needed to be written down. It is likely that Peter spoke and John Mark acted as secretary and that the Gospel of Mark was the result of their work.

BUT WHAT KIND OF BOOK?

I WANT A BOOK WHICH WILL HELP ME TO LIVE IN ROME AS A CHRISTIAN.

I WANT TO BE ABLE TO READ ALL THE EXCITING THINGS WHICH JESUS DID AND SAID.

LIFE IS HARD FOR CHRISTIANS IN ROME. I AM LOOKING FOR A BOOK TO ENCOURAGE ME WHEN TIMES ARE HARD.

And so Peter and Mark wrote a book which would meet the needs of these people. The second Gospel was written:

TO INFORM
The gospel answers the kind of questions that new converts would ask.

- How the Jesus story began (Mark 1:1–20)
- What impression Jesus made at the start (Mark 1:21–2:5)
- How a good man made enemies (Mark 2:6–3:6)
- How Jesus displayed his power (Mark 4:39; 6:56)
- Events leading to the death of Jesus (Mark 11:1–15:41)
- Jesus is really alive! (Mark 15:42–6:19)

TO INSTRUCT
Jesus expected his followers to live differently from others. His teaching covered a wide range of practical topics like:

- Fasting (Mark 2:18–22)
- Use of God's special day (Mark 2:23–28)
- Divorce (Mark 10:1–12)
- The importance of children (Mark 10:13–16)
- The Christian's attitude to money (Mark 10:17–31)
- Paying taxes (Mark 12:13–17)

TO INSPIRE
A large part of Mark's Gospel is about the sufferings of Jesus. Jesus suffered on behalf of his people and as an example to them. It must have been hard to be a Christian, to live with the threat of persecution and death hanging over you. Mark includes some encouragement for Christians who may find it necessary to suffer for what they believe to be true.

- Jesus was misunderstood (Mark 3:20–30)
- The danger of giving up (Mark 4:1–20)
- The cost of being a disciple (Mark 8:31–38)
- You must be different (Mark 9:50–51)
- The need to watch and pray (Mark 14:32–38)
- Jesus gives you power (Mark 16:14–18)

WE'RE THE GREATEST!

THE PHARISEES

The Pharisees saw themselves as God's special people. Their name, meaning 'the separated ones', marked them out as different. 'We alone obey God's ten commandments right down to the minutest detail', they claimed. The trouble was that in their efforts to help people keep the law of Moses, they added hundreds of small rules, some of which were handed on from one generation to another by word of mouth.

The Pharisees tried their best to keep these rules and looked down on those who did not.

THE SCRIBES

The scribes were the real experts in the Law of Moses. If you had any questions about this law, the scribes were the Masterminds with all the answers.

- They were teachers of the law. Their pupils were expected to pass on what they learnt without changing it in any way.
- They were legal advisers to the Jewish court, the Sanhedrin. (See page 96)

THE SADDUCEES

There were fewer Sadducees than Pharisees but their influence was greater. Most of them came from wealthy families. They also enjoyed positions of power. Almost half the seats on the Sanhedrin were filled by Sadducees.

But as far as their religion went, there were certain beliefs which they could not accept.

The Sadducees said:

- There is no life after death.
- There are no angels or demons.
- There are no rewards or punishments for the way you live.
- Only the first five books of the Old Testament are important. The rest can be ignored.

Most of the Pharisees, the scribes and the Sadducees did not get on with Jesus and argued with him when he was teaching.

Jesus criticised the Pharisees for doing things so that people would see them: 'Look at the straps with scripture verses on them which they wear on their foreheads and arms and notice how large they are! Notice also how long are the tassels on their cloaks!'

'You make up laws to suit yourselves. You do not really want to obey God', Jesus said. (Mark 7:9–13)

'You are more concerned with keeping rules than with loving God', Jesus said. (Luke 11:42)

'Jesus' power does not come from God. It comes from Satan', they accused. (Mark 3:22–30)

'Jesus actually chooses *sinners* for his friends', they grumbled. (Mark 2:15–17)

JOHN THE BAPTIST

'Large crowds have again gathered on the banks of the River Jordan in the Judean desert. People have travelled long distances to listen to a young preacher known simply as John. His appearance is striking. His preaching is powerful. Already there is much controversy surrounding this man of the desert . . .'

'I can remember the day young John was born. His father and I were great friends. Both Zechariah and Elizabeth used to spend time in our house. They loved playing with our children. You see they had none of their own. It came as a shock – but a pleasant one – to know that they were going to have a baby. Zechariah could not tell anyone the news. It wasn't until the baby had been born that he told me the whole story. He had been struck dumb by God for a time because he had disbelieved him.' (See Luke 1:5–25)

'I was one of John's first disciples. I knew there was something different about him the first time I heard him speak. He was so fearless it reminded me of the old prophets. There had been no prophet for four hundred years but when John spoke it was as though God himself was speaking.
    I suppose it was partly John's outspokenness that brought about his death. He told King Herod that he was wrong to have married his brother's wife, Herodias. She had it in for him after that. She put Salome up to ask for John's head. A few of us took his body and buried it. So young, so sad.' (See Mark 6:14–29)

'I was one of the people who was baptized by John. As he spoke I felt so wicked. I wanted to be forgiven. He told me to confess my sin and be baptized. I remember that day so well. As I came up from the water I felt so clean. It was like the first day of a new life for me.' (See Luke 3:10–14)

'You couldn't call me religious, not even in the broadest sense of the word. I went out to listen to John out of curiosity, I suppose. Strange looking character, was John. None of your fine clothes. A camel's skin and a leather belt. Reminded me of the stories my old dad used to tell me about the prophet Elijah.' (See Mark 1:4–6)

HIS MESSAGE

John's message could be summed up in four words:

> 'REPENT AND BE BAPTIZED'
>
> (See Luke 3:1–14).

REPENT

Repentance involved three things:

Seeing themselves as God sees them. And that's not a pretty sight.

Turning their backs on their old way of life and coming to God to say sorry.

Showing that they really had come back to God by living a new kind of life.

BE BAPTIZED!

John baptized people in the River Jordan.

A person who was baptized by John was saying:

> I WANT PEOPLE TO KNOW THAT I HAVE REPENTED OF MY SINS.

> I WANT TO START A NEW LIFE.

> I WANT TO STAND BY JOHN AND HIS TEACHING.

HIS MISSION

John made it very clear to those who listened to him that he was only a 'number two' preparing for a 'number one'. 'I am preparing the way for someone who is much greater than I,' John said. 'I baptize you with water but he will baptize you with the Holy Spirit.'

John always wanted to direct attention away from himself and to Jesus. He said he wasn't even good enough to untie Jesus' sandals and wash his feet. That was a job kept for the least important servant in any household (Matt 3:11).

KING HEROD AND JOHN

King Herod listened to John's preaching but he was disturbed by what John said. John kept telling him that he was wrong to marry his brother's wife, Herodias. Herod imprisoned John to keep him quiet. In his lonely prison John was puzzled by reports about Jesus but Jesus sent him a message to reassure him (Matt 11:1–6).

The sad story of Herodias's plot to have John beheaded and Herod's weakness is told in Mark 6:14–29.

WHAT DID JESUS THINK OF JOHN THE BAPTIST?

- Jesus came to John to be baptized. This showed people that he approved of John's work (Matt 3:13–17).
- Jesus called John the last of the prophets through whom God spoke (Luke 16:16).
- Jesus said John was greater than any man who has ever lived (Matt 11:11).

JESUS THE TEACHER

> MRS SCOTT IS GOOD. SHE MAKES EVERYTHING EASY TO UNDERSTAND.

> I LIKE MR WISEMAN. YOU CAN TELL THAT HE ALWAYS KNOWS WHAT HE'S TALKING ABOUT!

> MR TINGLEY'S A GOOD TEACHER. HE'S ALWAYS ABLE TO GRAB YOUR INTEREST.

WHAT MAKES A GOOD TEACHER?

We would all probably agree on some points. A good teacher, for example will be able to:

- Convince us that he knows what he is talking about.
- Hold our interest so that even at the end of a hot summer's afternoon our minds will not wander too far.
- Explain things in a way that makes sense to us.

JESUS WAS A GOOD TEACHER

If we look at the accounts of Jesus' work, it soon becomes clear that he was a very good teacher.

- When Jesus spoke, it was obvious that he knew what he was talking about. People were amazed because he had no special training like the religious teachers had.
- People were so interested in what Jesus had to say that sometimes they forgot what time of day it was! One day over five thousand people had listened all day and forgot they had no food with them. Jesus worked a miracle to feed them. (Matt. 14:13–21)
- People could understand what Jesus was saying, even when they might have preferred not to!

SOME WAYS IN WHICH JESUS TAUGHT

The unforgettable saying

Can't get those words out of my mind.

'Whoever wants to save his life will lose it but whoever loses his life for me and for the gospel will save it' (Mark 8:35).

The funny saying

I smile when I remember what Jesus said.

'Why do you look at the speck of sawdust in your brother's eye and pay no attention to the plank in your own eye?' (Matt 7:3).

The exaggerated saying

At first I couldn't believe Jesus meant it.

'It is much harder for a rich person to enter the Kingdom of God than for a camel to go through the eye of a needle' (Luke 18:25).

Jesus taught in a variety of places such as on a hillside, from a boat, in homes and synagogues and in the temple at Jerusalem.

THE PARABLES STARTED WHERE THE PEOPLE WERE

They were stories about the everyday life of those who were listening.

Jesus spoke about farming and fishing, fathers and sons, weddings and funerals, parties and games, housework and journeys. Right from the start people knew what Jesus was talking about.

One day he told the story of *The Lost Son.* (See Luke 15:11–32)

5 What a fool I've been!

6 I'll go back home and ask to be a servant.

1 Father, give me my share of the property.

7 Father, I'm sorry. I was wrong.

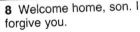
world now. 2 I'm off to see the

8 Welcome home, son. I forgive you.

3 Who cares? Let's have a good time.

4 My money's all spent. My friends have gone.

THE PARABLES TOOK PEOPLE TO WHERE GOD WANTED THEM

Jesus didn't tell stories simply to amuse the crowds. Each parable had a lesson that Jesus wanted the people to learn. In this story he was teaching them that God was like the father; he would forgive them if they were sorry for doing wrong.

Not everyone understood the lesson. Some only heard a good story.

Another day he told them a parable about a farmer who was sowing corn. (The story is in Luke 8:5–8)

After he had told this story his disciples asked him to explain it to them. He explained that the seed is the word of God which is sown in people's minds. Then the devil makes some of them forget what they have heard. Others believe but give up when it gets difficult or because they have too many other things to do. Only a few really hear God's word and obey it.

LUKE
MEET THE SAVIOUR OF THE WORLD

Luke wanted everyone to know that God loved them.
It didn't matter
• about their nationality
• about their importance in other people's eyes
• about the kind of life they had lived in the past.
And so Luke selected incidents in the life of Jesus which showed him to be the Saviour of the world who cared for everyone.

SAMARITANS
Some people, thought the Jews, are easy to love. When it came to their neighbours, the Samaritans, it was not so easy. Relationships between Jews and Samaritans had been bad for over 400 years. Both hated each other. Luke, however, shows that Jesus couldn't share these views even if they were held by one of his disciples (Luke 9:51–55). He also includes the story of the Good Samaritan (Luke 10:30–37) and the Samaritan who said thank you (Luke 17:11).

GENTILES
The Jews were quite pleased with themselves. They felt that they were God's favourites. And that made them quite different from all other nations, who were known as Gentiles. God, Jews thought, was not interested in Gentiles. But God was more loving than any human person. After all, as Jesus reminded them, God fed a Gentile woman (Luke 4:25,26) and healed a Gentile soldier (Luke 4:27). Jesus sent his disciples to share the good news of God's forgiveness to all nations (Luke 24:47).

'The Spirit of the Lord is upon me because he has chosen me to bring good news to the poor. He has sent me to proclaim liberty to the captives and recovery of sight to the blind; to set free the oppressed and announce that the time has come when the Lord will save his people' (Luke 4:18,19).

THE NEEDY
Jesus cared for those whom few others cared for. The poor were important to him. It was the rich who refused the invitation to the party but the poor who came (Luke 14:12–14). It was the beggar rather than the rich man who went to heaven (Luke 16:19–22).

LUKE'S GOSPEL
Written for non-Jewish readers by a former doctor who became Paul's friend and companion.

THE OUTCASTS
There are some people, said the Jews, whom you should avoid, unless, of course, you wish your reputation to be as bad as theirs. Such people were called simply 'sinners'. The Jews had no time for them. They were sure that God had no time for them. But, as Luke shows, Jesus did! He welcomed them, talked with them and shared meals with them. See Luke 5:27–32; 7:36–50.

WOMEN
'Thank you, God, that I am not a woman.' That was part of a male Jew's daily prayer and showed that women were second to men in their thinking. But Luke shows that women played an important part in the work of Jesus. Elizabeth, Mary and Anna all appear in the stories about the birth of Jesus. The widow who lived at Nain (Luke 7:11), Martha and Mary (10:38), Mary Magdalene (8:2) as well as the women at the tomb of Jesus (23:55) are all included in Luke's story of Jesus.

JESUS' BIRTH AND CHILDHOOD

The birth of Jesus was unique. God was definitely in control directing events.

- God decided the time of birth (Gal 4:4).
- God chose the woman to have the baby and the man to be her husband (Matt 1:20, Luke 1:30–32).
- God created the baby. Mary was a virgin and conceived the baby by the power of God (Matt 1:18).
- God chose the name for the baby (Matt 1:21).
- God chose the place of birth (Matt 2:3–6).
- God decided how to announce the birth (Matt 2:2, Luke 2:8).

The gospels tell us very little about the childhood of Jesus. We do know, however that:

- Jesus was brought up in Nazareth, a small village where nothing of importance usually happened (John 1:46).
- While living there Mary and Joseph had more children who, unlike Jesus, were conceived in the normal way (Mark 6:3).
- Like all Jewish boys Jesus probably learned a trade. Since Joseph was a carpenter, Jesus is likely to have worked in his workshop. Villagers later described him as 'the carpenter' (Mark 6:3).
- Jesus may have played the games that children in his village normally played (Matt 11:17).

Only one incident is described in any detail – Jesus' visit to Jerusalem at the age of twelve. It was an exciting time for him. A boy of twelve was considered ready for adulthood and this Passover would have been the first great festival he attended as a 'man' not a boy. The story in Luke chapter 2, verses 41–52, helps us understand Jesus as a young man:

- He was interested in talking about God.
- He had a good understanding about God.
- He was beginning to understand who he was and why he had been born.
- He was a good son to Joseph and Mary.

A Jewish boy's entry to adulthood is marked by a barmitzvah ceremony at the age of thirteen. This barmitzvah is in Jerusalem.

JESUS KNOWS WHAT IT'S LIKE TO . . .

- Live in a family.
- Have to share with brothers and sisters.
- Help around the house with the odd jobs.
- Play with friends who don't always agree.
- Be tempted to do wrong (Heb 4:15).
- Do as mum or dad says.

When we pray about these things Jesus understands!

JESUS THE HEALER

IMAGINE OPENING YOUR MOUTH AND HEARING YOURSELF SPEAK. AND BEFORE YOU MET HIM YOU WERE DEAF AND DUMB.

ONE MINUTE EVERYTHING WAS IN DARKNESS. THE NEXT MINUTE I COULD SEE.

THE FEVER SUDDENLY LEFT ME. I FELT SO GOOD I STARTED TO COOK THE LUNCH.

'TAKE UP YOUR BED AND WALK,' JESUS SAID. I DID.

HE TOUCHED ME – A LEPER. AND I WAS HEALED!

HE HEALED US

HE TOOK HER HAND AND SUDDENLY SHE WAS ALIVE.

In all four Gospels we find stories about Jesus healing people who were ill and even bringing dead people back to life. This power marked him out as different from other religious teachers of his day. It showed that he had the power of God.

The people Jesus healed were ordinary people. Here are some stories, based on the gospels.

A LEPER

'Nobody wanted to come near me because I had leprosy. I had to live on my own outside the town. One day I heard about Jesus healing people so I decided to risk going to town to try to get near him. What a crowd there was – all following him around to watch him and listen to him. They soon cleared a path when they saw me coming! I fell on my knees in front of Jesus and begged him to help me.

'If you want to, you can make me clean,' I said.

Jesus stepped forward and actually touched me!

'I do want to,' he answered with a kind smile. 'Be clean!'

At once I was healed! My skin was clear.

I was so happy I wanted to rush around and tell everybody. But Jesus told me to go to the priest and offer the sacrifice to show I had been healed.'

PETER'S MOTHER-IN-LAW

'I was in bed with a fever when Peter brought Jesus here. Jesus just reached out his hand to me and lifted me up. I could feel the strength coming back – just like that! I jumped up and got busy making dinner for us all.'

CHECK OUT THESE STORIES TOO
☐ A deaf and dumb man is healed (Mark 7:31–37).
☐ A blind man sees again (Mark 8:22–26).
☐ A paralysed man walks (Luke 5:18–26).
☐ A twelve year old girl comes back to life (Matthew 9:18–26).
☐ A Roman officer's servant is healed (Luke 7:1–10).

SPECIAL INVESTIGATION REPORT...

SUBJECT: *Jesus of Nazareth*

INVESTIGATION: *His power of healing*

THREE OF A KIND

Jesus' healings were one of three kinds:
- Disease
- Casting out spirits
- Raising from the dead.

Must get more information on this.

BACK FROM THE DEAD

Three dramatic stories:
- Widow who lived at Nain. (Son was raised to life on the way to his own funeral Luke 7:11-15).
- Jairus, a leader in one of the synagogues. His daughter was brought back to life just after her death. (Matthew 9:18-26).
- Lazarus - a must, this man! Dead three days and rotting in the grave yet brought back to life. (John 11:38-44).

CASTING OUT SPIRITS

Do some more research on this. Discovered that:
- Jews believed in existence of invisible spirits
- they seek entrance to body or mind and
- cause physical or mental illness.
- Healing brought about by casting out these spirits. NB. Look up stories on visits by Jesus to Capernaum and Gadara (see Mark 1:23-27 and Matthew 8:28-34).

HOW DID HE DO IT?

In different ways at different times.
- with a word ... the story about the break-in through the roof! (Luke 5:18-26).
- by touch ... his friend Peter's mother-in-law, and the leper. (Mark 1: 30-42).
- with feeling ... compassion, sometimes humour or anger. (Luke 7:11-15).
- with helps to faith ... spittle and clay. (John 9:1-7).

STRANGE BUT TRUE!

Seems Jesus unwilling to get a reputation as a healer. Actually told those he healed not to tell others about their healing. Didn't heal out of desire for publicity but out of love and compassion. Perhaps he wanted to be known as a teacher more than as a healer.

LUKE THE DOCTOR

Luke was a Gentile by birth whose first language was Greek.

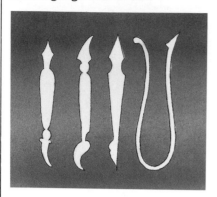

Luke received a good education which prepared him for a career in medicine. The Greeks were advanced in medicine and surgery. Four hundred years earlier a famous Greek doctor, Hippocrates, had laid down rules for doctors' behaviour which are still in use today. From his teaching, Luke would have learned to put the life and welfare of the patient first.

The Bible gives us no information about how Luke practised medicine. We know that there were both private and state doctors in Greece in his day. His Gospel shows his interest in medicine; he gives more details about diseases than the other writers.

Luke may have come into contact with Christians at Antioch where there was an active church. He was perhaps one of the 'great number of people' who 'believed and turned to the Lord' (Acts 11:19–21).

AD51 was a red letter year in Luke's life. He met the apostle Paul. From then on the two of them became both friends and fellow workers (2 Tim 4:11). He kept a diary of their travels (Acts 27. Note 'we . . .').

A fruit and vegetable market in Antioch.

Luke was later able to use his experience, his knowledge and skills to write two books. Together they would tell people the good news about Jesus and how it was passed on after he left his disciples. Volume one is called 'The Gospel of Luke'; Volume two is called 'The Acts of The Apostles'.

Tradition tells us that Luke continued to serve God faithfully until he died in Greece at the age of 84.

God still calls some men and women to 'change careers' as Luke did. One of the most famous preachers and writers this century was a doctor at one time. Dr Martyn Lloyd-Jones was told that a post was going to be offered to him that was so important that it would take him to the top of his profession. Dr Lloyd-Jones, however, turned it down. 'I had already decided for the ministry,' he said.

JOHN
MEET THE SON OF GOD

JOHN'S GOSPEL

Written about AD 90 for Christians in Asia Minor to help them to think through some of the things Jesus said and did.

John had a real problem. There was a limit to the number of pages in his book. But there was no limit to what he could write about Jesus. So how was he to decide what to include in his book and what to omit?

John told his readers about his problem.

'Jesus did many other miraculous signs in the presence of his disciples which are not recorded in this book. But these are written that you may believe that Jesus is the Christ, the Son of God, and that by believing you may have life in his Name' (John 20:30–31).

'Jesus did many other things as well. If every one of them were written down, I suppose that even the whole world would not have room for the books that would be written' (John 21:25).

John describes his PURPOSE in writing to help people understand that Jesus is the Son of God.

Of all the miracles which Jesus performed, John chose just seven. Each of them is like a signpost. It points not only to what Jesus did but to who he was and still is — the Son of God.

JESUS OF NAZARETH.

WHO IS HE, SIR, THAT I MAY BELIEVE IN HIM?
(John 9:36)

JESUS CHANGED WATER INTO WINE. JOHN 2:1–12.

JESUS HEALED AN OFFICIAL'S SON. JOHN 4:43–54.

JESUS HEALED A LAME MAN. JOHN 5:1–17.

JESUS FED FIVE THOUSAND. JOHN 6:1–13.

JESUS WALKED ON THE WATER. JOHN 6:16–21.

JESUS HEALED A BLIND MAN. JOHN 9:1–34.

JESUS RAISED LAZARUS FROM THE DEAD. JOHN 11:1–44.

JOHN
WORD PICTURES OF JESUS

I AM

said Jesus to some Jews who were questioning who he really was (John 8:48–58). But did he mean 'I am' just as 'you are' or 'she is'? Or did he mean something more?

When Moses was about to go back to Egypt on God's orders, he asked God a question. 'If people ask me for the name of the God who has sent me', he said to God, 'what name shall I give?' God's reply was short, 'Tell them that *I AM* has sent you.' So 'I AM' is God's name. Jesus is saying 'I am God.' These word pictures tell us something more about him.

THE BREAD OF LIFE

'**I am the bread of life**' (John 6:35). Jesus had just worked a miracle to feed 5000 hungry people with five loaves and two fish. They all followed him, hoping to see more miracles. But Jesus tells them that bread won't give them a God-filled life that lasts for ever. Believing in him will give them everlasting life.

It's a puzzle really. One day you read of the stars in their big houses, with their large cars and bank balances. The next thing you know, they are taking an overdose to escape from life. They don't seem to have found the secret of real living, do they?

THE GATE FOR THE SHEEP

'**I am the gate for the sheep**' (John 10:7). The people listening to Jesus knew all about sheep and shepherds. They knew that the sheep were herded inside an enclosure at night and the shepherd stayed in the only gateway to protect his flock.

Jesus is saying that he is the only way in to God.

We were talking in school the other day about becoming a Christian. Some of my friends said that going to church, doing your best, being christened or baptized made you a Christian. I didn't agree with them. After all the very name Christian tells you it's something to do with Jesus Christ. They seemed to have left him out of the picture.

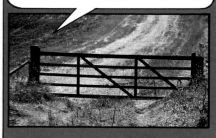

THE LIGHT OF THE WORLD

'**I am the light of the world**' (John 8:12). In Jesus' day there were no street lights to show the way at night. It was important to carry a lamp to see by. Jesus meant that if they listened to his teaching and obeyed him they would see how to live.

I'm beginning to wonder what life is about. Is it just a matter of exam success, good career prospects and a big salary? And then there are the big questions that seem to be bothering people today. There seem to be so many people who claim to have the answers. To be honest I feel at times I'm in the dark.

THE GOOD SHEPHERD

'**I am the good shepherd**' (John 10: 11).

Being a shepherd was a risky business. Robbers lay in wait to steal the sheep, wolves and other wild animals roamed the hill ready to pounce. A good shepherd would protect his sheep even if it cost him his life.

Jesus is saying that he is there to protect his followers from death. He stops life being wasted.

Ever feel that you're a nobody? I do. Just one insignificant, unknown nobody. I feel like that in a crowd at a soccer match or walking around the shopping precinct. I don't like the feeling. After all most of us want to be known, loved, cared for and protected, don't we?

THE WAY, THE TRUTH AND THE LIFE

'**I am the way, the truth, and the life** – no one goes to the Father except by me' (John 14:6).

The disciples were worried. Jesus had told them he was going away from them and they did not know where he was going to. Jesus explained that he was going to God. If they trusted him they were trusting God. No one else could get them to God.

We've been studying other religions at school: Islam, Hinduism, Buddhism, and a lot of others too. Some people say that all religions lead to God. 'We are all going in the same direction', they say, 'but along different paths.' But how can they be sure all the paths end up at the same place?

THE RESURRECTION AND THE LIFE

'**I am the resurrection and the life**' (John 11:25).

Jesus' friends, Mary and Martha, were very sad because their brother, Lazarus, had died. Jesus is saying to Martha that he can overcome death! To prove it, he brought Lazarus back to life again. Jesus promises life in heaven after death to all who trust him.

I heard my mum talking about a neighbour who had 'passed away'. Funny how adults don't like using the word death, isn't it? Or is it? Pretty morbid subject after all. I'd like to think there's life after death. I can't believe that we're thrown on the scrap heap like an old car. But how do we know?

THE VINE

'**I am the vine**, and you are the branches' (John 15:5).

Vines grew on the sunny hillsides of Palestine and they are often mentioned in the Bible. Jesus was telling his disciples that just as a branch on its own away from the vine is no good so they needed to stay with him in order to be like him.

There are times when I hate myself. I know what kind of person I would like to be. But I just can't make it work out in my life. That's why I admire Jesus. I'd love to be like him, but how?

TRIAL, DEATH AND RESURRECTION

PALESTINIAN ECHO

SATURDAY

Golgotha witnessed the death yesterday of a man who brought life and hope to many.

After repeated efforts to free the teacher from Nazareth, Pontius Pilate finally gave in to the demands of the Jewish leaders.

After a scourging, the young teacher was marched through the streets to the skull-shaped hill outside the walls of Jerusalem. There Roman soldiers followed their practice of execution by crucifixion. Crowds watched as the cross was hoisted into the air before being dropped into the ground. Two thieves were crucified with him.

Some of his followers, mostly women, wept as they watched him die. Some of those who had pressed Pilate to have Jesus killed, stood laughing and jeering.

Fear gripped many, however, when at noon darkness suddenly came upon the

PALESTINIAN ECHO

READ ALL ABOUT IT!
- ☐ The Arrest of the Teacher (Mark 14:43–50).
- ☐ The Trial before the Jews (Mark 14:53–65).
- ☐ The Trial before Pilate (Mark 15:1–15).
- ☐ The Execution (Mark 15:21–41).
- ☐ The Burial (Mark 15:42–47).
- ☐ The Resurrection (Mark 16:1–7).

PALESTINIAN ECHO

FRIDAY

END OF THE ROAD FOR THE NAZARENE?

Jesus of Nazareth is dead. The man who rode into Jerusalem cheered by the crowds, walked to Golgotha today and to his execution.

As a result of a secret plot which involved one of his closest friends Jesus was arrested in Gethsemane. His trial before the Jewish Court, the Sanhedrin, leaves a number of questions unanswered. What charge was brought against him? What evidence was produced to prove his guilt?

Reliable sources suggest that after a number of unsuccessful attempts to bribe witnesses, the High Priest broke the rules of the Court by asking the defendant a direct question.

'Are you the Christ, the Son of the Blessed One?'

There was a hush in the court. His reply, 'I am' brought cries of 'Blasphemy! Kill Him!' Beaten by the

PALESTINIAN ECHO

SUNDAY

MYSTERY OF THE MISSING BODY!

Tonight mystery surrounds the body of Jesus of Nazareth, the young teacher who was executed on Friday.

Following a request to Pontius Pilate, permission was given to Joseph of Arimathea, a member of the Jewish Court, to take the body of Jesus for burial in his own garden tomb.

Investigations revealed that witnesses are available to confirm that the body was taken from the cross, wrapped in bandages and placed in the tomb. A large stone was then rolled across the entrance. It is also clear that Roman soldiers were placed on guard outside the tomb at the request of the Jewish leaders. They seem to have feared that attempts might be made to steal the body of Jesus.

Early this morning, however, women who came to the tomb to anoint the body with spices found the stone rolled away, the bandages lying on a ledge in the tomb but the body gone. Reports are coming in of sightings of Jesus by both men and women. Followers of Jesus claim that he is now alive!

Whatever the truth of the situation, one thing is clear. The body is missing and with nobody able to produce it, the claims of these disciples remains unchallenged. Is Jesus alive today?

THE END? — NO, JUST THE BEGINNING

WAS JESUS' DEATH A TERRIBLE MISTAKE?
Jesus had given hints about his death to his disciples, (see Matthew 16:21) but they did not really understand why he had to die until afterwards. After Jesus had gone back to heaven, the disciples began to tell everyone the good news of God's offer of forgiveness of sin because of Jesus' death. The writers of the book of Acts and the New Testament letters explain the importance of Jesus' death and resurrection and show how it was foretold in the Old Testament. See Acts 2:22–42 for example.

THE LAMB OF GOD
In Old Testament times, people had to bring a lamb to the priest who killed it as a sacrifice for their sins. Jesus was called the Lamb of God (John 1:29). His death brings forgiveness of sins to all who believe in him. Once Jesus had died there was no need for any more sacrifices.

THE EMPTY TOMB
The resurrection of Jesus showed that he had conquered death.

Paul explained, in his letter to the Corinthians, how that affects all Christians:

'But the truth is that Christ has been raised from death, as the guarantee that those who sleep in death will also be raised' (1 Corinthians 15:20).

THE TORN CURTAIN
In the Temple there was a heavy curtain across the entrance to the Holy of Holies, the part particularly set aside for God. The ordinary people were forbidden to enter there. Once a year the High Priest went in past the curtain to offer a sacrifice on behalf of the people. When Jesus died on the cross that heavy curtain tore from top to bottom, showing that the way to God was open to everyone.

AND TODAY — SO WHAT?

'During those extraordinary minutes of history, Jesus, who had no sin of his own and could therefore be absolutely at one and in harmony with his Father, took on the sin of the whole of humanity. Your sin and mine, everything that spoils and drags us down, was nailed there with Jesus.

'Forget the world's sin. That's too huge a concept to comprehend. Just imagine Jesus dealing with yours. That would have been cause enough for God to turn away and for Jesus to experience his isolation.

'I'm no theologian and couldn't begin to answer all the questions about what happened at Calvary, but I know myself, and I know what I deserve from a God who is perfect and demands perfection. I'm only grateful, and want my life to be a 'thank you' to the God who now accepts me as perfect because Jesus wiped the slate clean when He became 'my sin' on the cross.'

You, Me and Jesus. Cliff Richard (Hodder & Stoughton, 1983)

THE ACTS OF THE APOSTLES
SPREADING THE GOOD NEWS
STAGE 1

| AD 20 | 40 | 60 |

/PENTECOST

In the Gospels we read about Jesus' life and death. The Acts of the Apostles begins with Christ's Ascension. (See below) Then, fifty days later, at Pentecost God sent his Holy Spirit to give the apostles power to spread the good news over all the earth.

The last recorded words of Jesus in Matthew's gospel are:

> 'Go then to all peoples everywhere and make them my disciples; baptize them in the name of the Father, the Son and the Holy Spirit . . . and I will be with you always to the end of the age.' (Matt 28:19–20)

The last recorded words of Jesus in Acts are:

> 'When the Holy Spirit comes upon you, you will be filled with power and you will be witnesses for me in Jerusalem, in all Judea and Samaria and to the ends of the earth.' (Acts 1:8)

The book of Acts describes how these words were carried out.

THE AUTHOR OF ACTS
The book of Acts is anonymous – but there are some clues in Acts chapter 16.
- In v. 1 it says *Paul* travelled
- In v. 4 it says *they* went . . . but
- In v. 10 it says *we* got ready.

So it looks as if the author joined Paul and his companions. When we compare Acts 1:1 and Luke 1:3–4, we see that both are addressed to Theophilus. So it looks as if the author of Acts was Luke who joined Paul on the second missionary journey.

CHRIST'S ASCENSION
Jesus has now returned to his Father. He has gone out of our sight – but we are never out of his sight.

You can read the story in Acts 1:6–11.

On earth Jesus could only be in one place at a time. He could not help different people in different places at the same time. But when he went back to heaven, God promised to send the Holy Spirit. The Holy Spirit is with *all* Christians, in *all* places, *all* the time.

EXPANSION
They will start preaching in Jerusalem.

Many Christians will be scattered through Judea (see p 98).

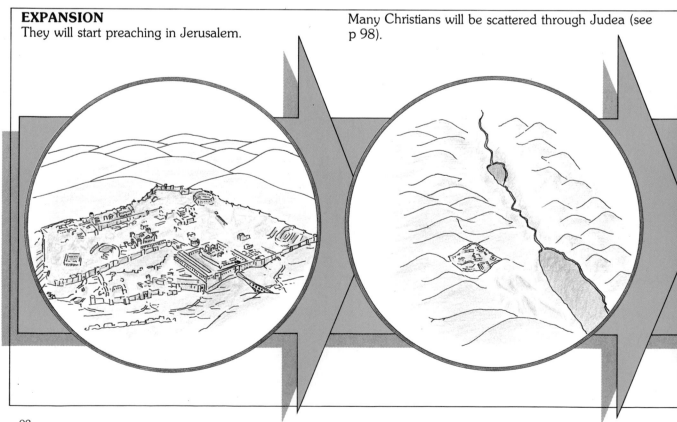

JESUS WILL RETURN

'This Jesus, who was taken from you into heaven, will come back in the same way' (Acts 1:11).

PENTECOST – SMALL BEGINNINGS

Just eleven frightened apostles, a group of women and some other believers, 120 in all . . . but Jesus had told them to preach 'to the ends of the earth'. How could they?

SPEAKING IN TONGUES

There was a great crowd of Jews in Jerusalem for the festival. The story in Acts 2:1–13 lists all the different countries they came from. The apostles, filled with the Holy Spirit, burst out of the upper room and began praising God. They went straight to the crowds and began to preach. But all the crowds were amazed to hear God's praises in their own native languages!

When they returned home, they too began the gospel expansion to their own people.

DRUNK AND DISORDERLY!

The authorities accused the apostles of being drunk – at 9 o'clock in the morning! No, they were not drunk. It was the Holy Spirit giving them power.

THE GROWTH OF THE CHURCH

After the coming of the Holy Spirit at the Pentecost festival, the church began to grow.

The word 'church' does not mean a building. There were no church buildings yet.

The word 'church' means the whole group or body of believers.

The church was growing very fast. Believers met in each other's houses.

They met to
☐ learn from the apostles' teaching
☐ encourage one another
☐ share in fellowship meals (communion)
☐ pray and worship

THEY SHARED EVERYTHING THEY HAD

There is a description of the early church in Acts 2:42–47.

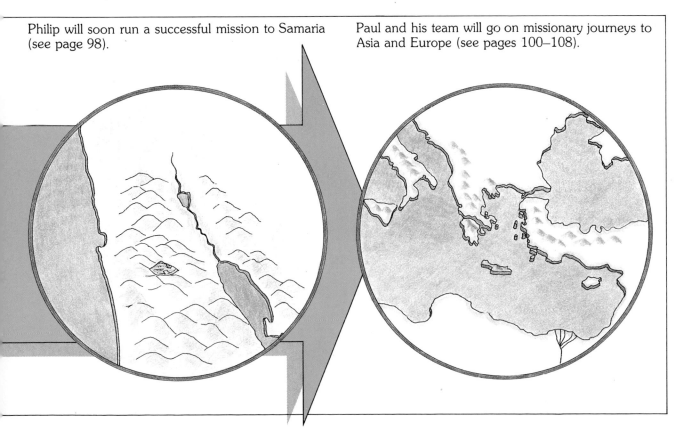

Philip will soon run a successful mission to Samaria (see page 98).

Paul and his team will go on missionary journeys to Asia and Europe (see pages 100–108).

GETTING THE MESSAGE ACROSS

The disciples had been told to 'be witnesses to the ends of the earth'. They were helped in getting the message across by the Jews, the Greeks and the Romans.

PAX ROMANA
The Romans had conquered most of the ancient world. Instead of being cruel to the conquered nations, they tried to make them their allies. They put Roman officials in charge, settled some retired soldiers on farms, then allowed the people to carry on in their own way (provided they paid their taxes). The result was peace in most of the Empire (Pax Romana in Latin). This meant that the first Christian missionaries who went to tell the good news of Jesus could go in peace from country to country.

ROMAN TRAVEL
The Romans made many improvements in travel, although compared with today it was slow, uncomfortable and even dangerous. Ships were small and were powered by sails and oars, normally sailing only in spring and summer. Carts and carriages had iron wheels and no springs, covering only a few miles a day.

The missionaries walked or rode on the fine roads; they also went by ship.

ROMAN ROADS
In the centre of Rome stood the Golden Milestone, from which went well-made roads in all directions, covering all of the Roman Empire. These roads were constructed by the army as they invaded each country. They kept them in good condition for trade and for the Emperor's special couriers.

The missionaries could travel from country to country on these roads.

ROMAN LAW AND ORDER
The Roman Governors enforced law and order in each country or province. Free people (not slaves) were protected by law and treated fairly. The missionaries could expect to be protected and treated fairly.

The Roman Empire

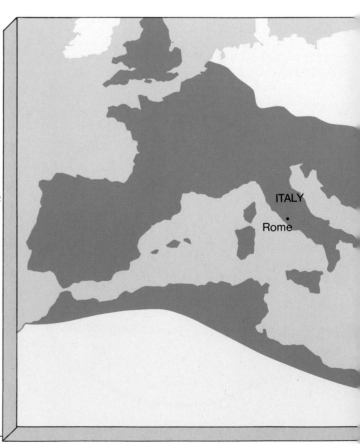

ITALY

Rome

ROMAN COINAGE
Roman coinage was used in all countries of the Empire. The missionaries did not have to worry about changing their money.

GREEK THINKERS
There was much fear and superstition. People carried out sacrifices to their gods because they were afraid. They did not ask questions about their gods. But the Greeks loved asking questions and discussing new ideas. Greek thinkers were called philosophers. Who am I? What is truth? What is a good person? How should I behave for the good of the state?

People were ready to listen to the missionaries and discuss the new religion.

GREEK LANGUAGE
The majority of people in the countries of the Roman Empire spoke Greek as a second language. So the missionaries did not have to learn new languages. They could pass on the good news about Jesus in Greek.

ROMAN CITIZENSHIP
Being a Roman citizen was like being a member of a club of very important people. Citizens had many privileges. They could not be imprisoned or flogged without trial. You could buy citizenship, or be given it as a reward. Paul was born a Roman citizen, so he could expect to be treated with respect.

THE JEWS
Throughout their history the Jews had suffered from attacks and persecution, so thousands had scattered from Israel and settled in all parts of the ancient world. Wherever they went they continued to worship God. They built synagogues.

Wherever the missionaries went they were sure to find groups of Jews, who believed in the true God and knew the Old Testament.

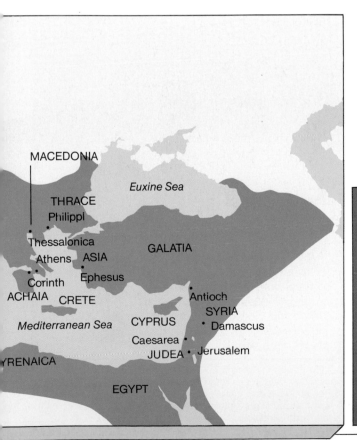

AT THE RIGHT TIME
God could have sent Jesus to earth at any time in history. He chose to send him in Roman times. As you can see from these pages, it was the best time. The missionaries could travel in peace. People were ready to listen to the good news about Jesus. Today missionaries are still busy getting the message across. But they are using many new methods:

- They can travel by aeroplane.
- They can send radio broadcasts right into areas that are closed to missionaries.
- They can use films, TV, videos and cassettes.
- They are still obeying Jesus' command to 'be witnesses to the ends of the earth.'

THE ACTS OF THE APOSTLES

SUFFERING FOR JESUS

TROUBLE

The church was growing fast. Many Jews, even some priests, had left the synagogue to join the church. This made the Jewish leaders furious. Some were jealous of the Christians' popularity and power.

Some were stubborn and refused to listen to the good news. Some were proud and would not admit they were wrong. They began to persecute the Christians and give them a bad time.

PERSECUTION BEGINS

1. Peter and John healed a lame man at the Beautiful Gate of the temple (Acts 3:1–10). Peter preached to the huge crowd that gathered.

2. The Jews were furious and arrested them. They warned them not to preach any more, then let them go. (Acts 4:1–22).

4. The Jewish Council† wanted to kill the apostles (Acts 5:17–42). They forbade them to preach, flogged them and let them go. Peter and John were happy that God considered them worthy to suffer for Jesus' sake.

3. Peter and the other apostles wouldn't stop, so they were put in prison. They were freed by an angel*! When the guards came to take them before the Council, the cell was empty! They found them back in the Temple court . . . preaching again!

*Angels are not people with wings and long white dresses. The Greek word *angelos* means messenger. God sends his heavenly messengers to earth from time to time:

- to inform or warn people (Genesis 19:1–22)
- to judge and destroy (2 Kings 19:35)
- to guide and instruct (Zechariah 1:8–17)
- to protect and help (Daniel 6:22)
  People usually recognize them at once.

†The Jewish Council, the Sanhedrin, had seventy elected members, under the High Priest, who was appointed by the Roman Governor. It dealt with political and religious matters and was also the High Court of the nation. It had no power to pass the death sentence.

STEPHEN – THE FIRST CHRISTIAN MARTYR

In those days the rich were very rich and the poor were very poor. So the believers decided to share everything (Acts 4:32–37). The apostles shared it out among those who were in need. But the Greek-speaking Jews complained that their widows were neglected. Peter did not feel it was right to give up preaching in order to sort out money and food.

SEVEN HELPERS

The believers prayed, then chose seven helpers to organise food and money matters. One of them was Stephen.

STEPHEN

Stephen began his task. He also preached and performed miracles. The Jews were jealous, so they arrested him on false charges. When he stood before the Jewish Council they saw that 'his face looked like the face of an angel' (Acts 6:15). He preached fearlessly to them about Jesus. Then he said, 'I see Jesus standing at the right hand of God'. The right hand of God is the place of power. Only God's chosen one (Messiah) can stand there.

With a loud cry the members of the Council covered their ears with their hands. Then they all rushed at him at once, threw him out of the city and stoned him. The witnesses left their cloaks in the care of a young man named Saul. They kept on stoning Stephen as he called out to the Lord, 'Lord Jesus, receive my spirit!' He knelt down and cried out in a loud voice, 'Lord! Do not remember this sin against them!' Then he died. (Acts 7:57–60)

MARTYRS

Stephen was the first Christian martyr. Since then thousands of other Christians have died for their faith.

AN UNFINISHED TASK

In spite of opposition, the good news about Jesus has been taken to people throughout the world since New Testament times. This diagram shows there are still many more people who need to hear the good news.

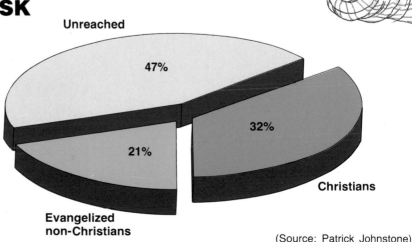

Unreached 47%

32% Christians

21%

Evangelized non-Christians

(Source: Patrick Johnstone)

THE ACTS OF THE APOSTLES

SPREADING THE GOOD NEWS
STAGE 2

TO JUDEA

'You shall be witnesses for me in Jerusalem, in all Judea and Samaria and to the ends of the earth' (Acts 1:8).

After the stoning of Stephen, the cruel persecution of Christians in Jerusalem continued (Acts 8:1–4). Life became so difficult and dangerous that Christians were forced to leave. They scattered throughout Judea . . . and they told the people there about Jesus.

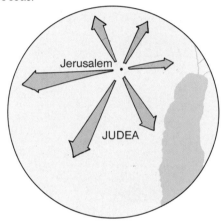

TO SAMARIA
The Jews had despised the Samaritans for centuries. Now the Jewish Christians wanted to share the good news with everyone – even Samaritans.

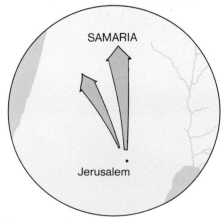

PHILIP
When Philip fled from Jerusalem, he went to Samaria and led a mission there, preaching and performing miracles. It was a great success.

There are two Philips in the Bible:

1. Philip, one of Jesus' twelve apostles, a Jew.
2. Philip, the evangelist, a Greek, who appears in this story. Like Stephen he was one of the seven helpers (see p. 97) chosen to help the apostles. You will find his name in Acts 6:5.

PHILIP AND THE ETHIOPIAN

In the middle of Philip's successful mission to Samaria, an angel told Philip to go to Gaza . . . in the middle of the desert! There he saw on the road a chariot approaching. In it there was an Ethiopian, Chancellor of the Exchequer to Queen Candace of Ethiopia. He was a God-fearer (see p 104) returning from a festival in Jerusalem and reading a scroll, which he could not understand. You can read the whole story in Acts 8:26–40.

Philip explained that the verses on the scroll, from Isaiah, referred to Jesus, who died for his sins. The Ethiopian believed and was baptised.

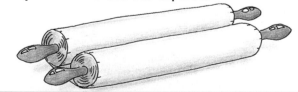

SPREAD THE GOOD NEWS TODAY

Millions of people still have not heard the good news about Jesus, even some of our neighbours. God does not expect everyone to run missions or stop people in their cars – or chariots! But all Christians should be ready to share the good news whenever and wherever they can.

PAUL – THIS IS YOUR LIFE

FROM SAUL THE JEW . . .

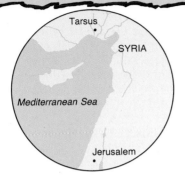

. . . TO PAUL THE CHRISTIAN

Saul grew up in Tarsus, in Asia Minor. His parents, who were Roman citizens, were strict Jews, so he was circumcised on the eighth day. They named him Saul. They taught him the Jewish Scriptures. He was brought up as a Pharisee (see p 77). He moved to Jerusalem to attend the University. He studied under Gamaliel, a famous teacher.

He kept up his violent threats of murder against the followers of Jesus. He tried to destroy the church by throwing the believers into jail. When he finished in Jerusalem, he set off for Damascus to arrest the followers of Jesus there.

Saul was totally changed. Now he put all his energy into preaching about Jesus. The Jews in Damascus were furious – they expected him to stamp out Christianity, not preach about Jesus! They plotted to kill him. His unusual way of escape is described in Acts 9:23–25.

SAUL OR PAUL?

His parents called him Saul, a Jewish name. When he was on his missionary journeys he began to use his Roman name – Paul.

Paul is famous for:
- Preaching and teaching
- Missionary journeys (see pp 100 and 106)
- Letter writing. Paul wrote thirteen of the epistles (letters) in the New Testament.
- Suffering. He was beaten, stoned, imprisoned, shipwrecked and often in danger. There is a vivid account of his sufferings in 2 Cor 11:23–29.

Saul was positive that Jesus was not the Messiah. When he heard what Stephen said about Jesus (p 97) he was furious. When the Jews stoned Stephen, Saul approved of his murder and held their coats for them.

On the Damascus road he had a vision of Jesus in blazing light. Jesus called him by name. The light blinded him, so his friends led him to Damascus. (The story is in Acts 9:1–20.)

For three days he sat without eating or drinking. He was praying. A disciple called Ananias laid hands on him and he regained his sight. He was filled with the Holy Spirit and was baptized.

THE ACTS OF THE APOSTLES, GALATIANS
SPREADING THE GOOD NEWS
STAGE 3

| AD 40 | 50 | 60 |

/PAUL'S FIRST JOURNEY

MOVING OUT . . .
- The Holy Spirit was now at work, giving power to the Christians.
- There was now a lively, growing church in Jerusalem. (p 102)
- Many Christians had scattered throughout Judea, spreading the message.
- After Philip's mission (p 98), there were churches in Samaria. Now for the world!

OFF YOU GO, PAUL (Acts 13:1–3)
The church in Antioch, in Syria, had many leaders. The Holy Spirit told them to send Barnabas and Paul (Saul – see p 99) off to take the good news to other countries.

They laid their hands on them, as a sign that they were going as their representatives to do God's work.

FIRST STOP CYPRUS
Cyprus was the home of Barnabas. As they preached first in the synagogue, they met Elymas Bar-Jesus, a magician, who tried to stop the Roman Governor from believing – read about his punishment (Acts 13:4–12).

WHERE NEXT?
There were so many people – villages, towns, provinces, countries – who had never heard about Jesus. Paul had a plan of campaign:

to preach. Many Jews became Christians.

3. Opposition. When Jews believed, they left their synagogues. Those who were left were furiously jealous. They often attacked or persecuted the missionaries. Read about some of the ways that Paul suffered in 2 Cor 11:24–28. But he still went on, because he loved Jesus.

4. To the Gentiles. When the Jews of Pisidian Antioch attacked him Paul said, 'We leave you and go to the Gentiles.' Paul was known as the apostle to the Gentiles.

5. Second visits. He tried to return to strengthen and encourage the Christians.

6. Home again. (Acts 14:27–28). A great church meeting welcomed them back. Paul told them, 'God has opened the way for the Gentiles to believe'.

7. Keeping in touch. Paul longed to see the new converts, but was often too busy to revisit them – or in prison for preaching. So he wrote letters, sometimes called epistles, which are included in the New Testament. The earliest was probably the one written to the Galatians. Several were written from prison.

1. He chose key towns, in the centre of Asia Minor (Turkey), so the new believers could spread the word.

2. To the Jews first. Paul was a Jew and cared deeply for his people (Read Rom. 10:1). He always went first to the synagogue

Paul's first journey

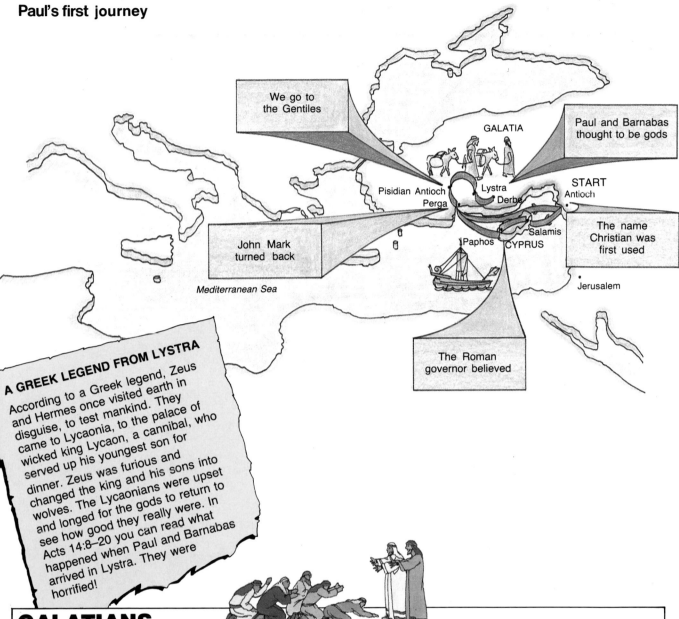

We go to the Gentiles

Paul and Barnabas thought to be gods

GALATIA

Pisidian Antioch
Perga

Lystra
Derbe

START
Antioch

John Mark turned back

Salamis
Paphos
CYPRUS

The name Christian was first used

Mediterranean Sea

Jerusalem

The Roman governor believed

A GREEK LEGEND FROM LYSTRA

According to a Greek legend, Zeus and Hermes once visited earth in disguise, to test mankind. They came to Lycaonia, to the palace of wicked king Lycaon, a cannibal, who served up his youngest son for dinner. Zeus was furious and changed the king and his sons into wolves. The Lycaonians were upset and longed for the gods to return to see how good they really were. In Acts 14:8–20 you can read what happened when Paul and Barnabas arrived in Lystra. They were horrified!

GALATIANS

After Paul returned from the first missionary journey he was worried about all the new Christians. So he wrote a letter to the group of churches in Galatia – this included the area of Lycaonia with the towns of Iconium, Lystra and Derbe. It was probably written in AD 47 shortly after Paul's visit. Most of the new believers were Gentiles – but they had a problem:

- I am surprised at you (Gal 1:6).
- I am very worried about you (4:20).

- You foolish Galatians, who has put a spell on you? (3:1)

What had happened? When Paul first preached, the Gentiles had listened eagerly and many had believed. BUT . . . since Paul's visit, other Jewish teachers had arrived, with false teaching. They said:

- To follow Jesus you must be circumcised.
- If you want to be a Christian, you must keep *all* the Jewish Laws.

These false teachers said: You are slaves to the Law.

But Paul said, 'No! Christ has set us free from having to follow all the regulations in the Law. He wants us to love him and to let his Spirit direct our lives.'

Paul describes how this works out in Gal 5:22,23. He calls it the fruit of the Spirit. Christians should pray that the fruit of the Spirit will be seen in their lives.

BACK AT HEADQUARTERS

JERUSALEM

Millions of tourists go to Jerusalem . . . why? Jerusalem is the historical centre of two world religions – Judaism and Christianity. Judaism is the religion of the Jews, who are all descended from Abraham, the first Jew. They are known as 'God's chosen people'. God chose them and prepared them to expect and welcome the Messiah, but they rejected Jesus as their Messiah.

THE CHURCH IN JERUSALEM

In Jerusalem there were no Gentiles, except the occupying force of Romans and a few traders. So the church was made up of Hebrew Christians – Jews who now believed that Jesus was the Messiah. They still kept their Jewish beliefs and worshipped in the temple, until it was destroyed in AD 70.

The church in Jerusalem was

- **An important church**, whose members included some of the apostles, James the brother of Jesus, Silas, John Mark and many important women.
- **A persecuted church.** The strict Jews were furious when other Jews became Christians. As Christians, they were no longer allowed to attend the synagogue. This meant they could not join in public worship. Other Jews would not speak to them, trade with them or employ them.
- **A suffering church.** There was a famine, so the Christians were in great need. Some Gentile churches had collections to help them. 1 Cor 16:1–3.

GOD'S CHOSEN PEOPLE

The Jews were taught that they should be separate from Gentiles. In order to keep themselves separate and to keep their religion pure, they had many rules and regulations. This meant that they were different from all the other nations.

ISRAEL

Today we think of Israel as a place. But Israel is also another name for the Jews.

NAMES FOR THE JEWS

HEBREWS
since the time of Shem (Genesis 10:21).

ISRAELITES
(or children of Israel) since Jacob received the name Israel (Genesis 30:28).

JEWS
since the time of the Exile in Babylon (Daniel 3:8).

ISRAELIS
since 1948 for those Jews who returned to their land, Israel.

A street in Jerusalem.

COVENANT
God made a special agreement (covenant) with Abraham, promising to bless his descendants, the Jews.

SEPARATION
Strict Jews would not willingly enter a Gentile's house, or ever eat with Gentiles. They were allowed to marry other Jews only.

CIRCUMCISION
This is a small operation done on Jewish boys at eight days old. The loose skin, called the foreskin, at the tip of the penis is cut off. It is a sign that a boy is a Jew.

LAW
Jewish beliefs are contained in the writings, known as the Law. The Law, including the Ten Commandments, is found in the first five books of the Old Testament. In Old Testament times Israel was the only nation that gave free education, to boys aged seven to thirteen. They had to know their Law, and why they were different from other nations.

FOOD LAWS
Jews were allowed to eat the meat of only certain animals, known as 'clean' animals. See Leviticus 11. This probably began as a health rule. Pigs are on the list of 'unclean' animals, so Jews do not eat pork. Jewish food, particularly meat, must be killed and prepared in a special way called 'Kosher'. 'Clean' animals are killed by cutting the windpipe and letting the blood drain out.

TEMPLE
The Jews' great joy was to visit the temple (see pages 40/41). There they worshipped God and made sacrifices. Although the first Christians still worshipped in the temple, they did not make sacrifices. Jesus' death on the cross was the only sacrifice that was needed for the sins of the world.

A scroll of the Law (above left) is still read as part of the synagogue service.

THE ACTS OF THE APOSTLES
GOD WANTS GENTILES TOO

Jesus was a Jew. The apostles were Jews. The first Christians were Jews. Jesus' last recorded words were:

'You will be witnesses for me to the ends of the earth' (Acts 1:8).

So the good news about Jesus was meant for Gentiles as well as Jews.

JEWS AND ROMANS
☐ The Jews and Romans hated one another.
☐ The Jews saw the Romans as their conquerors, who had invaded their land.
☐ The Romans found the Jews unco-operative and very difficult to handle.

JEWS AND GENTILES
☐ A Jew is someone born of a Jewish mother.
☐ A Gentile is anyone who is not born a Jew.
☐ A proselyte is someone who accepts all the beliefs of Judaism. He is circumcised and agrees to keep all the Jewish Law.
☐ A God-fearer is someone who accepts all the beliefs of Judaism but he is not circumcised and does not agree to keep all the Jewish Law.

THE STORY OF CORNELIUS (Acts 10)

The very first Gentile Christian that we know by name was Cornelius, one of the Roman invaders. He lived in Caesarea, a Roman-style town and was an officer in the Roman army.

One day, while Cornelius, a God-fearer, was praying, God spoke to him in a vision, telling him to go to Joppa to fetch Simon Peter.

DAY 1

GO TO JOPPA!

DAY 2

While Peter was praying on the roof top, he had a strange vision of a huge sheet, full of animals. He heard a voice telling him to kill and eat.

Peter was shocked, as they were unclean animals that Jews were not allowed to eat. But God said, 'Do not consider unclean anything God says is clean'.

Meanwhile, Cornelius sent two servants and a soldier, a religious man, to find Peter at the house of Simon the tanner.

At first Peter wasn't going to have Gentiles in the house – but then he understood *God has no favourites* – he accepts Gentiles as well as Jews.

Peter went to Caesarea. He entered a Gentile house! As he preached, Cornelius and his family believed. They were baptized and received the Holy Spirit.

DAY 3

GOD HAS NO FAVOURITES

Cornelius received the Holy Spirit. This proved that God does accept Gentiles as well as Jews.

God still has no favourites. He loves everyone equally:

- ☐ the Jews
- ☐ the poor
- ☐ the good-looking
- ☐ the young
- ☐ the slow ones
- ☐ the Gentiles
- ☐ the rich
- ☐ the ugly
- ☐ the old
- ☐ the clever ones

God wants everyone to love him.

THE COUNCIL OF JERUSALEM (Acts 15)

Many Christians, like Peter and Paul, had preached to Gentiles. As they travelled, they saw that God had given the Holy Spirit to Gentiles. So they wanted to let Gentiles join the new church, without being circumcised or agreeing to keep all the Jewish Law.

But the church in Jerusalem was made up of Jewish Christians. They did not want 'unclean' Gentiles in their church, or in their homes. They insisted that Gentiles must be circumcised and agree to keep all the Jewish Law.

There were fierce arguments between the two sides. To solve the matter, a meeting was held, called the Council of Jerusalem. Peter, Paul and others made speeches. Peter said, 'God showed his approval of the Gentiles by giving the Holy Spirit to them, just as he had to us.'

Paul reported all the miracles God had performed among the Gentiles.

As a result, James, a leader of the church in Jerusalem, said that Gentiles could be accepted as Christians without being circumcised or agreeing to keep *all* the Jewish Law.

So the Council wrote a letter to the churches.

Greetings to our brothers and sisters of Gentile birth. We do not want to burden you with too many rules, only these:

- Do not eat food that has been offered to idols.
- Live pure lives, having sexual relations with your marriage partner only.
- Do not eat meat unless the blood is drained out.

With our best wishes, James, the apostles and elders in Jerusalem.

Jews and Gentiles could therefore enter each other's houses and eat together.

Jews and Gentiles could share bread and wine at communion.

When the letter was read to the Gentile believers they were glad and encouraged.

THE ACTS OF THE APOSTLES
WESTWARD TO EUROPE

AD 40   50   60

/PAUL'S SECOND JOURNEY

SECOND MISSIONARY JOURNEY

After the first missionary journey Paul had left new Christians in charge of the new churches. He had written a letter to some of them (the Galatians, see p 101). But he still longed for news of them. So he decided to visit them again.

Paul prepared to set off, taking Barnabas with him. But Barnabas wanted to give John Mark another chance, after he had deserted them on the first journey (Acts 13:13). Paul disagreed, so after a sharp argument they split up. Paul took Silas with him.

Barnabas took John Mark with him to Cyprus.

But God had even more exciting plans for Paul.

Paul planned to visit Asia, a Roman province in Paul's time, part of Turkey today.

God planned for Paul to go to EUROPE.

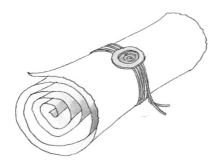

There were no postmen in those days. Letters had to be carried by hand. News was brought by travellers. The Emperor had special couriers.

IN PHILIPPI

Paul preached to people from very different backgrounds, like these people from Philippi.

☐ Lydia was a rich woman, who sold very expensive purple dye. She already worshipped God, so she listened very carefully to Paul's preaching and became a Christian. She invited the missionaries to stay at her home (Acts 16:11–15).

☐ This poor slave girl had an evil spirit in her. She could predict the future. Her owners forced her to tell fortunes, so they could become rich. Paul healed her. Read Acts 16:19–22 to see what the owners thought of that!

☐ The brutal jailer who guarded Paul and Silas was amazed to hear them singing hymns at midnight! His exciting story is in Acts 16:19–34.

The Parthenon, the temple of the goddess Athene, would have been seen by Paul on his visit to Athens.

1. At first Paul did not realise that God wanted him to go to Europe. After he had revisited Derbe, Lystra, Iconium and Pisidian Antioch, he thought he would visit other towns in Asia Minor (Turkey).

2. In Lystra Paul met a young man called Timothy. He decided to take him with him in place of John Mark. (see p 108)

3. He was longing to spread the good news in Asia – in Mysia, Phrygia, and Bithynia. But the Holy Spirit somehow stopped him from preaching and urged him on towards the west, until he reached Troas – a dead end! Then in the night he had a vision of a man from Macedonia asking for help (Acts 16:6–10).

MACEDONIA IS IN EUROPE

4. Philippi. (see p106)

5. In Thessalonica a large group of Greeks believed. The Jews were jealous, so they caused a riot. Paul had to leave (Acts 17:1–9).

6. In Berea the people listened eagerly and studied the scriptures every day.

7. In Athens Paul was disturbed to see so many idols. There was even an altar to an unknown god. Only a few Athenians believed. They thought themselves too clever to believe in Jesus, particularly his resurrection (Acts 17:16–34).

8. Paul spent one and a half years in Corinth. Many Corinthians believed (Acts 18:1–18).

9. Paul travelled across the Aegean Sea to Ephesus, taking Priscilla and Aquila with him (see p108). He left them there. The people of Ephesus wanted him to stay longer, but he wanted to return home to Antioch.

10. Instead of going straight back to Antioch, he went first to Jerusalem and greeted the church there. His ship landed at Caesarea, a fine city built by Herod the Great, in Roman style.

11. Home at last!

Paul's **second** journey

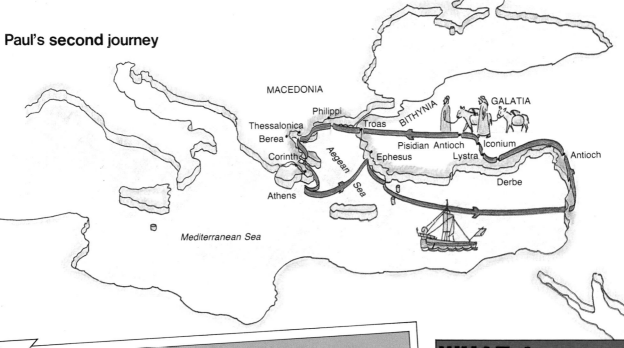

WHAT A DIFFERENCE!

Being a Christian makes a difference to the way people behave. It made a difference to Lydia – she opened her home to the missionaries, although other people considered them unwelcome troublemakers. It made a difference to the jailer. He was a tough, brutal man who often flogged his prisoners. Now he took Paul and Silas to his own home and washed their wounds.

TEAMWORK

Paul did not work alone. He was part of a team, with all members pulling together. Read about some of his team and pick out their special abilities.

LUKE

Luke, who wrote Acts, was the only New Testament writer who was not a Jew. He was a Greek doctor, living in Asia Minor. He joined Paul on the second missionary journey and looked after Paul, who was often ill. He was an excellent historian, who checked all the facts before he wrote his Gospel and Acts (Col 4:14, 2 Tim 4:11).

Troas
Luke joined Paul

Ephesus
Timothy's church
Priscilla and Aquila's house church

BARNABAS

Joseph Barnabas was a Jew from Cyprus. He sold his lands and gave all the money to the church. His special gift was encouraging others. When Paul first came to Jerusalem, only Barnabas welcomed him. So the apostles gave him the nickname 'Barnabas' which means 'Encourager'. He specially encouraged his young cousin John Mark, taking him with him to work in Cyprus (Acts 4:36–37, Acts 9:26–27).

PRISCILLA AND AQUILA

When Priscilla and Aquila were living in Rome, the Emperor Claudius expelled thousands of Jews, in AD 49. They moved to Ephesus as Aquila was a Jew. Priscilla, who is always mentioned first, was probably a Roman. As Christians their gift was hospitality and Paul stayed with them several times, even helping them with their tent-making. They opened their home as a meeting place for believers and were full of love for their Christian brothers and sisters (Acts 18:1–4, Rom. 16:3–5).

SILAS

Silas, a member of the Jerusalem church, was both preacher and prophet. His church chose him to go to Antioch to welcome the Gentiles into the church family. As a trusted helper, he accompanied Paul on his second journey, always backing him up. Peter called Silas 'a faithful Christian brother'. At the time he was helping Peter to write his letters (p 127), Peter preferred preaching – or fishing – to writing, so Silas was very useful (Acts 15:30–34, 1 Peter 5:12).

TIMOTHY

Timothy's grandmother and mother, who were Jewish, had taught him the Old Testament scriptures. His father was a Greek. When Paul visited Lystra on the second journey (p 107) he decided to take the young Timothy. Paul loved him as a son and trained and encouraged him. During the third missionary journey Paul left Timothy at Ephesus, as church leader. Paul wrote two letters (p 120) to help and challenge him, praising him for his sincere faith and his knowledge of the scriptures (Acts 16:1–3, 1 and 2 Timothy).

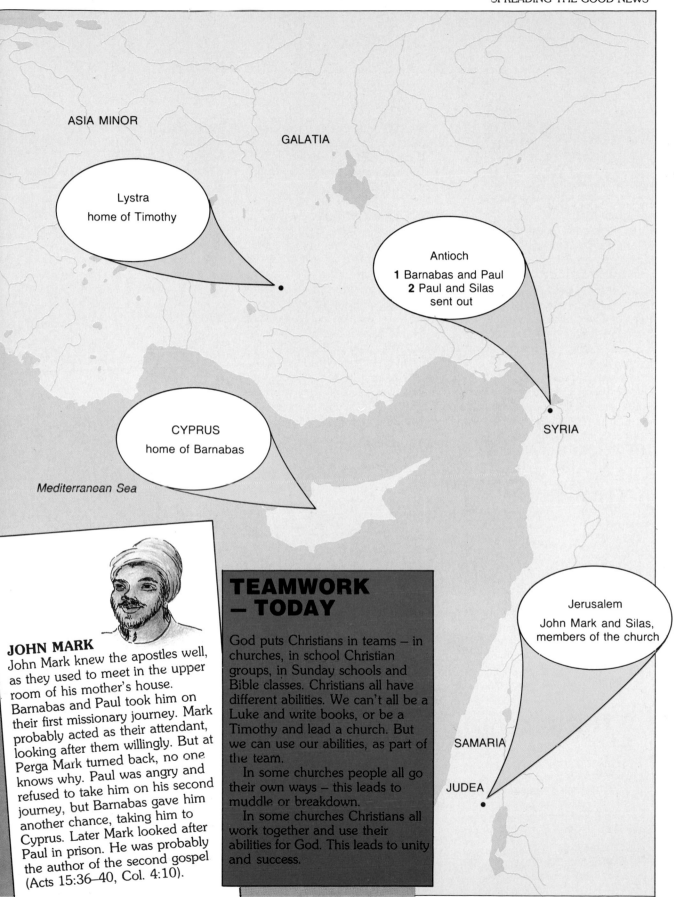

ASIA MINOR

GALATIA

Lystra
home of Timothy

Antioch
1 Barnabas and Paul
2 Paul and Silas
sent out

SYRIA

CYPRUS
home of Barnabas

Mediterranean Sea

Jerusalem
John Mark and Silas,
members of the church

SAMARIA

JUDEA

JOHN MARK

John Mark knew the apostles well, as they used to meet in the upper room of his mother's house. Barnabas and Paul took him on their first missionary journey. Mark probably acted as their attendant, looking after them willingly. But at Perga Mark turned back, no one knows why. Paul was angry and refused to take him on his second journey, but Barnabas gave him another chance, taking him to Cyprus. Later Mark looked after Paul in prison. He was probably the author of the second gospel (Acts 15:36–40, Col. 4:10).

TEAMWORK – TODAY

God puts Christians in teams – in churches, in school Christian groups, in Sunday schools and Bible classes. Christians all have different abilities. We can't all be a Luke and write books, or be a Timothy and lead a church. But we can use our abilities, as part of the team.

In some churches people all go their own ways – this leads to muddle or breakdown.

In some churches Christians all work together and use their abilities for God. This leads to unity and success.

1 AND 2 THESSALONIANS, 1 CORINTHIANS
VISITS AND LETTERS

TROUBLE AT THESSALONICA

PAUL WAS NOT ALWAYS WELCOME!

Riots broke out when he had been at Thessalonica for only three weekends, preaching in the synagogue and at Jason's home, and Paul had to be sent away for his own safety (Acts 17:1–10). Persecution of the Christians carried on after he left, and he worried about the church – would it survive the test?

He sent Timothy on a fact finding mission. He brought good news and Paul wrote to them with joy and thanks to God, and again a few months later to encourage them.

We call these two letters 1 and 2 Thessalonians. Why did Paul write to them?

ENCOURAGEMENT

'Well, first I wanted to reassure them that I was praying for them as they struggled on, thanking God for them all the time.

Then I reminded them of the message I had taken to them and mentioned that I'd like to visit them to teach them more. However, as I couldn't come right away I wanted to help them to live for Jesus, bearing in mind that he is coming back soon! They must be ready for him all the time, and not be ashamed of anything they do.'

MISUNDERSTANDINGS

'I should have made this clearer because some of them misunderstood what I had written about Jesus coming back. They thought they could sit back and not do any work because Jesus was on his way any day now – and they were teaching others their ideas! So I wrote the second letter to put that right. It isn't going to be easy while we wait for Jesus to come, it will be a battle all the way.'

THESSALONICA – now
Thessaloniki – was the capital city of the province of Macedonia. It was near Mount Olympus, the centre of many pagan myths and religions. The city had a successful port, stood on a major Roman road, and drew visitors from all over the Roman Empire.

THE CHURCH WAS ALIVE AND GROWING!

1 THESSALONIANS

'We always thank God for you all and always mention you in our prayers. For we remember before our God and Father how you put your faith into practice, how your love made you work so hard, and how your hope in our Lord Jesus Christ is firm' (1 Thess 1:2–3).

'May the Lord make your love for one another and for all people grow more and more . . . in this way he will strengthen you . . .' (1 Thess 3:12–13).

2 THESSALONIANS

'Our brothers, we must thank God at all times for you . . . because your faith is growing so much and the love . . . is becoming greater (2 Thess 1:3). Do not be so easily confused . . . by the claim that the Day of the Lord has come . . .' (2 Thess 2:3).

'. . . pray for us, that the Lord's message may continue to spread . . . the Lord is faithful, and he will strengthen you and keep you safe from the Evil One' (2 Thess 3:1–3).

WHO WILL STOP THIS MADNESS?

WE CALL UPON THE MAGISTRATES of our noble city to put an end to this disgusting new religion called Christianity. Executing their leaders Paul and Jason would certainly please Zeus. The people showed their feelings today when they dragged Jason, one of their leaders to the magistrate for trial . . .

1 CORINTHIANS

WORRIES ABOUT CORINTH

Paul had worked as a tent-maker and missionary at Corinth for a year and a half. The church grew despite the struggles. Later, Paul wrote to help them in their problems and encourage them.

DIVISIONS (1 Cor 1–4, 9:12–14)

The Christians disagreed over leaders; many rejected Paul himself. They weren't working together as a team either. Paul showed that the local church is like a body; all the parts working together for Jesus and love holding them together. (Read chapter 13)

PRESSURES (1 Cor 5–7, 10–11)

There were strong temptations to conform to the greedy, selfish and evil ways around them. Living for Jesus seemed like running up a 'down' escalator – tiring, not much point in it, and not the 'normal' thing to do.

Paul urged them to be faithful in marriage, unlike most of the city, (1 Cor. 7:2) and to avoid greed and drunkenness – which occurred even at communion! (1 Cor. 11:20–22).

MISUNDERSTANDINGS (1 Cor 8)

Meat sacrificed to the gods was sold in temple butchers and temple restaurants. Some Christians had no problem about buying it – meat was meat and these 'gods' were just lumps of stone. Others felt it was right to make a complete break with their old lifestyle, including buying meat from temple butcher shops. Paul warned those who felt free to buy this meat not to cause problems for others (1 Cor 8:9–10).

DEATH (1 Cor 15)

Many had forgotten how important Jesus' resurrection was. Paul reminded them that this was *the most* important fact in the Christian life, giving certainty and victory to every believer!

CORINTH

Many of the people living at the port of Corinth were very rich – they had time and money on their hands to spend at entertainments and debates. They were keen on art, philosophy and language study, but their culture and luxury led them into wickedness. The city became a 'by-word' for evil! Much of it centred on the worship of the Greek goddess, Aphrodite.

Christians have always faced persecution, not only at Thessalonica or Corinth. In the early days many Christians were burned alive or made to fight lions.

The temple of Apollo at Corinth was built in the sixth century BC.

IT HAPPENS TODAY

'Ian constantly annoyed me at school – picking fights, ganging up, putting obscene books in my desk – mainly because I was a Christian. It was miserable. A few years later, after we had left school he contacted me. "I've become a Christian," he said, "and the main reason was the way you stood up to what I did." I didn't know it, but God was using me all along!'

ROMANS AND 2 CORINTHIANS
OFF AGAIN

| AD 50 | 60 | 70 |

/PAUL'S THIRD JOURNEY

TRAVEL DIARY

Left Antioch for Galatia and Phrygia, visited
Christians. Acts 18.23.

Spent two years at Ephesus, wrote to
Corinthian Christians, left soon after the riots.
Acts 19.

Into Macedonia, Titus arrived with good news
from Corinth, wrote to the church at Corinth
again. Went on to Achaia – stayed three
months. Wrote to church at Rome, returned to
Troas via Philippi – met up with Timothy and
friends. Acts 20:1-6.

To Miletus, near Ephesus. Met leaders from the
church at Ephesus and encouraged them. Acts
20:13-38.

Returned to Jerusalem visiting Christians on the
way; warned at Tyre that I was heading for
imprisonment. Took relief money to starving
Christians at Jerusalem. Acts 21:1-17.

Paul stayed at Ephesus for two years, hiring a lecture hall to preach in. The Christians made such an impact on the city that the silversmiths were unable to sell their statues. You can read about the riots in Acts 19. Many of the people who practised witchcraft gave up their old ways, burning their books as they left their old way of life and let Jesus take over.

Paul wrote his first letter to the Corinthians while he was at Ephesus.

WELCOME TO EPHESUS – home of the great
goddess Diana (called Artemis in Greek).
Population 300,000.
We have a great selection of temples to choose
from, to suit every taste – some dedicated to the
Emperor.
To make your stay more profitable (to us) do
purchase a model of Diana's temple – the largest
building in the Empire – and a statuette of Diana
herself.
Magicians are here to serve you and tell your
fortunes – special rates to tourists and soldiers in
the Imperial army.
Our theatre seats up to 25,000 and provides a
wide range of tempting entertainment.
Ships depart for all parts of the empire
from our port.

ROMANS

Paul had never been to Rome when he wrote to the Christians there. Other Christians had visited Rome on business, or for other reasons and talked about Jesus to their friends there. Many were Jewish Christians. Paul hoped to visit them and wrote to them from Corinth to let them know who he was and what his message was.

ROMANS IS ABOUT THE WAY GOD CHANGES PEOPLE

Romans 1–3. We have all failed God!
Romans 4–5. There is only one way to God – trusting in Jesus to be our Saviour.

'God has shown us how much he loves us – it was while we were still sinners that Christ died for us! By his death we are now put right with God . . .' (Rom 5:8–9).

Romans 6. We were 'dead' but now we're alive; we were slaves to sin but now we're slaves to God!
Romans 7. Though there is a struggle going on inside us – Paul tells us he often did what he knew was wrong . . .
Romans 8. . . . there is forgiveness available, and the Holy Spirit to help us to live for God . . . and the reminder that no one and nothing can separate us from God!

'. . . I am certain that nothing can separate us from his love' (Rom 8:38).

Romans 12–15. Some practical advice – how to go on helping and supporting each other.

2 CORINTHIANS

Paul wrote this letter while he was in Macedonia. He had heard that the Christians in Corinth were solving their problems (see p 111). But there were still things to be sorted out.
Help each other as God has helped you (2 Cor 1:1– 11;8–9).

'He helps us so that we are able to help others using the help we have received' (1:4).

Be strong – you have been made new people, friends of God, and have been given a message to share (2 Cor 5 and 6).

'. . . Christ changed us from enemies into his friends and gave us the task . . .' (2 Cor 5:18).

To those who couldn't accept Paul, he told his own story, what he had been through for Jesus and how Jesus had used him; though he didn't like talking about himself (2 Cor 10 and 11).

Paul's third journey

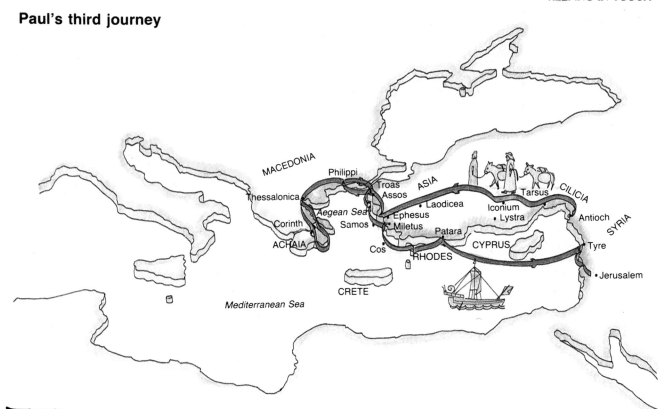

+PAUL + URGENT + STOP + FAMINE + AT + JERUSALEM + STOP + CHRISTIANS + STARVING + STOP + MONEY + NEEDED + FOR + FOOD + STOP + SUGGEST + COLLECTIONS + AT + CHURCHES + STOP + BROTHER + JAMES + STOP +

MISSIONARIES TODAY

Times have changed! Missionaries still go to other countries but they get there more quickly today.

Even when they need to cross the jungle or need medical help they can call the Missionary Aviation Fellowship. Their tiny planes can land on very small airstrips. A way has even been devised to lower and collect items in a container slung beneath a circling plane when no landing strip is available!

Other missionaries go over hostile territory by hovercraft. Land Rovers and motor bikes speed them on their way, and radio and TV help get the message to millions. BUT missionaries still

face many dangers! – see page 115.

They need your support – gifts, letters and prayers. One of your skills might be letter writing! How about becoming a pen-friend of someone whose parents are missionaries? Your church leaders could give you addresses and details.

TIMES CHANGE . . .
but the message is the same today!

'I have complete confidence in the gospel; it is God's power to save all who believe . . .' (Romans 1:16).

'Sin pays its wages – death; but God's free gift is eternal life in union with Christ Jesus our Lord' (Romans 6:23).

I APPEAL TO CAESAR!

PAULS' JOURNEY TO ROME

FIGHTING FOR THE TRUTH

Nero was a cruel dictator who ruled the Roman empire – and his family – for his own benefit. He loved flattery and received it from anyone who wanted to get on in life or even survive! Though Paul urged Christians to honour their human rulers, Nero tried to destroy the church. His chance came when Rome was burned down (possibly by Nero himself!) and he could blame the Christians. He had them rounded up and killed in cruel ways for the entertainment of the people of Rome.

Nero's armies began the war that ended in the destruction of Jerusalem in AD 70, though by that time he had killed himself.

2. Paul told the crowd how Jesus had changed him on the way to Damascus and sent him to share Jesus' message with people who aren't Jews (called 'Gentiles'). At this the crowd rioted and Paul was taken into the fortress to be flogged to get the full story. He was spared his flogging when he told the officers that he was a Roman citizen.

3. Paul was taken to the Chief Priest and the whole council (the Sanhedrin). There was almost a riot. God told Paul that night that he would be able to witness, not only in Jerusalem but in Rome itself.

1. Returning to Jerusalem, Paul reported to the church leaders and gave them the relief fund he had collected. Within a few days he had to be rescued by Roman soldiers from a mob in the temple. He was arrested partly for his own safety and partly because the Roman officers didn't know who to believe – Paul or the mob.

4. More than forty men plotted with the Sanhedrin to have Paul killed. The attempt was foiled. Paul was sent to Felix, the Governor at Caesarea, with a letter of explanation. (Acts 23:12–30)

5. After two years at Caesarea, the new governor, Festus, and King Herod Agrippa heard Paul. Agrippa felt Paul was even trying to convert him! Paul declared that he should have the right to appeal to the Emperor. Festus and Agrippa concluded, 'This man could have been set free if he had not appealed to the Emperor.'

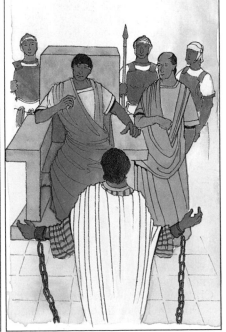

ROMAN CITIZENS

Children of Roman citizens inherited this privilege, but you could also buy it for a large sum of money, or earn it by special service in the army. A slave might become a citizen on being set free.

A Roman citizen could not be tied up or imprisoned without proper trial (Acts 22:29) nor could he be whipped. He could appeal to the Emperor for justice.

Paul's journey to Rome

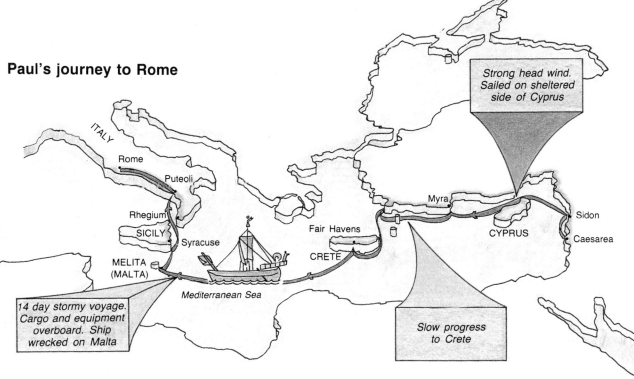

Strong head wind. Sailed on sheltered side of Cyprus

Slow progress to Crete

14 day stormy voyage. Cargo and equipment overboard. Ship wrecked on Malta

Mediterranean Sea

ITALY — Rome — Puteoli — Rhegium — SICILY — Syracuse — MELITA (MALTA) — CRETE — Fair Havens — Myra — CYPRUS — Sidon — Caesarea

TO ROME – CENTRE OF THE EMPIRE

It was late in the year to attempt a full sea voyage to Italy, but the officer decided to take the risk. They kept near the coast, arriving in Crete at the end of September. Trying to make for a safer harbour they were caught by a strong storm from the north-east and were blown away into the middle of the Mediterranean Sea. The storm carried them onwards for two weeks until they were wrecked on the island of Malta, where they stayed for the winter.

Arriving at Rome without further trouble, Paul spent two years under guard in a house where he could receive friends and write letters – and tell the guards about Jesus! (See Philippians 1:12–14).

WHAT HAPPENED AFTER THAT?

The rest of Paul's life is unknown. It is possible that he was released and went to Spain, as he had wanted (Romans 15:24,28), and other areas. Some think that he was killed at Rome alongside other Christians who were persecuted by Nero.

Paul was sure that he was being used by God all the time and he had no fears of God's judgement.

Why should he? His past life had been forgiven and God had used him to spread the good news.

> 'I have done my best in the race, I have run the full distance, and I have kept the faith. And now there is waiting for me the victory prize . . .' (2 Timothy 4:7–8).

Paul's journey to Rome was in a very small boat, at the mercy of the storm, but despite modern, safer methods of travel, missionaries still need prayer for safety. Driving on tracks and difficult roads brings danger. In 1978 twelve died in a minibus crash in Thailand, including seven children. Some have been victims of terrorist kidnapping or other attacks. Others have caught fatal tropical diseases or been in earthquakes.

You can read about modern missionaries and the dangers they face. Pray for others hard at work for Jesus.

EPHESIANS, PHILIPPIANS, COLOSSIANS, PHILEMON

LETTERS FROM PRISON

AD 50   60   /PAUL IN PRISON   70   /JERUSALEM DESTROYED

You might think Paul had quite enough on his mind to bother much about the churches he'd formed. Yet while under guard in a house near Rome he sent long letters to them.

Why did you bother with them, Paul?
'I really miss them, you know. They are a very important part of my life – almost like my family! I get concerned about what I hear about them and though they have God's help they still need to know I care.'

Did you ask for help, a hacksaw in a pie, perhaps?
'Oh no, I don't want to escape, in fact it would rather spoil the way God is working. You see, they keep changing the guards on the other end of these handcuffs and I talk to them, about all sorts of things, especially Jesus – and they can't get away. I reckon I've talked to hundreds of soldiers in the palace guard about him this way and some have been converted! It's a privilege to be here! But I do ask the churches for help – prayer help, it's the greatest help anyone can give.'

And how did you try to help the churches?
'By pointing them to Jesus. He can inspire them; his life and death, and the fact that he is alive again, are a great encouragement, and if they trust him for the strength of the Holy

Spirit nothing can stop them! They also need help in sorting out their relationships; wives and husbands, bosses and slaves, parents and children, dealing with anger, forgiving each other – the sort of daily problems anyone has to face.'

EPHESIANS

Find out more about Ephesus – see pages 112 and 131.
Eph 1. Dear brothers and sisters, I thank God for your good news, may God help you even more!
Eph 2. Remember – you were spiritually dead because you were away from God, now you're alive! – and all because God loves you, not because you did anything – that's grace.

'. . . it is by God's grace that you have been saved through faith. It is not the result of your own efforts, but God's gift . . .' (Eph 2:8–9).

He has made us all one people . . .
Eph 3. Jesus' love in our hearts is the key to that unity.
Eph 4. Put that love into practice. If God has made you one people, work together as one.

'If you become angry do not let your anger lead you into sin . . . don't give the devil a chance' (Eph 4:26–27).

Eph 5. Go on being filled with the

Holy Spirit. Work out how you can live with each other – wives and husbands, children and parents, masters and slaves.
Eph 6. Finally – put on all the armour God gives to defend you against Satan's attacks. You'll need it in that evil city of Ephesus.

'At all times carry faith as your shield . . . and the word of God as the sword which the Spirit gives . . . (Eph 6:1 and 17).

Pray for me too.
☐ Your friend and brother, Paul (signed)

COLOSSIANS

Paul had not been to Colossae (a town near Ephesus) but hoped to go there soon; (see Philemon). The population was a mixture: Greeks, Jews and people from Phrygia lived there, and probably many of these were Christians. They could be a threat to the purity of the teaching in the church, as they brought their own ideas from their old religions. (Phrygians were very loyal to their national god Cybele). So Paul wrote a lot in his letter about how to sort out the false from the true. Most of chapters 1 and 2 are about Jesus –

'Christ existed before all things, and in union with him all things have their proper place. He is the head of his body, the church; he is the source of the body's life . . .' (Col 1:18–19).

'Our lives must show that Jesus has changed us,' he said in chapter 3.

'You are the people of God; he loved you and chose you for his own. So then, you must clothe yourselves with compassion, kindness, humility, gentleness and patience' (Col 3:12).

. . . especially in the way we treat each other; wives/husbands, children/parents, slaves/masters – we should be one family in Jesus!

PHILEMON

Paul's messenger to Colossae was Tychicus (4:7), but he didn't go alone. Onesimus was a slave, owned by Philemon, a Christian at Colossae. He had run away and was converted through listening to Paul, who was sending him back with a personal letter. (See page 119 for more about that letter)

PHILIPPIANS

Philippi was the first European city where Paul preached. It was a major city of the area, and a gold mining area. It was famous for a battle in 42 BC and after that it became a Roman colony, its people having the same status as if they lived in Italy. Many of its people had lived in Rome or other important areas. Those who read Paul's letter would have understood what he meant by 'citizens' of heaven (3:20).

The young church at Philippi (see page 106) was special to Paul; though some were teaching wrong ideas, he knew God would carry on helping them;

'I am sure that God, who began this good work in you, will carry it on until it is finished . . .' (Phil 1:6).

Phil 1. They cared about Paul, and he wrote to say that he was still being used by God. He wanted them to learn more about Jesus and aim to live like him.

'The attitude you should have is the one that Christ Jesus had: . . . he took the nature of a servant . . .' (Phil 2:5–7).

Phil 3. Some wanted to go back to their old Jewish ways. Paul reminded them that following Jesus is much better.

'My old Jewish past is almost like rubbish compared with knowing Jesus,' he wrote in 3:1–11.

Phil 4. Filling our minds with good things, and doing the good things Jesus wants is the way to peace.

'Put into practice what you learnt . . . And the God who gives us peace will be with you' (Phil 4:9).

These cities and countries seem very far away, and the people lived in very different times. We don't wear togas and sandals, we aren't surrounded by temples to hundreds of gods. We forget that they faced the same sorts of problems as we do. They worried about what people thought about them, they were tempted to go back to the old life they once lived, they argued – sometimes about very little things, just like us!

The churches in those days weren't particularly 'better' than our churches today just because they were in the Bible. The letters which Paul and others wrote have just as much meaning for us as they did when they were written.

SLAVES – PEOPLE OR TOOLS?

SLAVES AS TOOLS

The Roman Empire was built on slaves! If the Romans had done all their own work, they would not have had time to enter politics, law, trade or the army. Rome would have remained a small power. By using slaves as their tools they had time to build their Empire.

Slaves were sold in the slave market, as though they were animals. They became the property of their owners, who could treat them as they pleased. They were not always ill-treated or over-worked.

But runaway slaves, if caught, were branded with FUG meaning runaway.

Thieves were branded FUR meaning thief.

The new churches, set up during Paul's missionary journeys, included both masters and slaves. Here are some examples of the kinds of slaves the Romans used.

MILO

Milo was captured in Gaul and trained at the Gladiator School. His job was to entertain the crowds, shedding as much blood as possible. He became a star with many fans. If he won often enough the Emperor might set him free. If he lost . . .

BREGANS

Bregans was captured by the Romans in Britain and taken to Rome. As he was uneducated he was sold as a farm slave and treated like an animal. He slept in an underground prison, with leg chains. He was quite well-fed as his master wanted to get the best out of him.

LILA

Lila's parents were slaves, so Lila was born into slavery. She was well-treated, as long as she worked hard. She was trained as a hairdresser, also doing make-up and massage. She saved her pocket money to buy her freedom, as slaves could not marry.

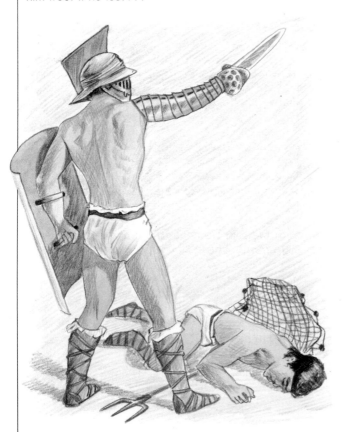

MARCIA

Marcia was born a free Roman, but her father sold her to pay his debts, when she was ten. As a household slave she was up early, worked hard all day, then late to bed. She was beaten for every fault. Her master was a monster who enjoyed the sound of whips and cries of pain. Marcia did not dare run away, but she wished she were dead.

PHILIP

Philip and his brother were well educated in Greece, but were kidnapped by pirates and sold for a good sum. Philip's brother was tutor to a Senator's son. Philip was a public slave, working for Rome and organising the water supplies. He received lots of money from bribes and would soon be able to buy his freedom.

KURM

Kurm was captured by the Romans during a war, and was sold. He refused to work. He was flogged and sold as a galley slave. He was chained to his oar. If the ship went down, he would probably go down with it. He was overworked, under-fed and often whipped. He had no hope of freedom.

PHILEMON

Paul wrote a letter to Philemon, one of his many Christian friends, who lived in Colossae.

☐ **The Background** Onesimus, one of Philemon's household slaves, had stolen some money and run away. Somehow he had met Paul, who was now in prison in Rome. Onesimus became a Christian through Paul.

☐ **In the letter** Paul calls himself Onesimus' 'spiritual father' Philm v.10. Paul had told him to go back to his master, but he was very frightened. So Paul gave him this letter. It begs Philemon to take Onesimus back 'as a brother in the Lord'. Read about Paul's generous offer in v.18–19.

PEOPLE – NOT TOOLS

'That slave's not working – don't give him any food.'

'But he's sick.'

'I don't want sick slaves – take him back to the slave market.'

'But . . .'

In Roman times slaves were treated as tools, not people. Today slavery is not allowed, thanks to people like William Wilberforce and Abraham Lincoln who led campaigns for slavery to be abolished last century. But it is still possible to use people like tools. Some people trample on others to get to the top. Sometimes the rich push the poor people around. The strong push the weak as though they don't matter. Jesus taught that everyone matters to God. 'Look at the birds flying around; they do not sow seeds, gather a harvest and put it in barns; yet your Father in heaven takes care of them! Aren't you worth much more than birds?' (Matt. 6:26). People must never be treated as tools.

TIMOTHY AND TITUS
PULLING TOGETHER

PAUL THE PASTOR

Paul wasn't a loner, he had a team to help him. On pages 108–9 we met some of his team-mates, but there were others who prayed, gave, advised, helped locally and so on.

'Paul, how do you feel about your team?'

'Confident! I can rely on my team – they're committed to Jesus all the way, and they rely on him, and he won't let them down.'

'But you had some difficulty with some of them, didn't you?'

'Yes, I did feel John Mark let us down badly at the time (Acts 13:13); I may have expected too much of the lad in my early days and I guess Barnabas helped him more (Acts 15:36–41). We've forgiven each other now and get on well together (2 Tim. 4:11).

Some were good starters but have gone back to their old ways. That saddens me. I know that, left to my own strength, I'd be the same; it's hard to live for Jesus.'

'What sort of team do you want around you, Paul?'

'First they must be people who know Jesus as their own Saviour and Lord, to stand firm when they're under attack. They must go on learning the Bible. They must try to live like Jesus too, like servants. I encourage them to build teams round themselves as well. Like me

they can't do all the work themselves. I'm sure Timothy and Titus will let you read my letters. That's the best way to find out.'

TIMOTHY AND TITUS

Timothy probably became a Christian at his home town, Lystra, during Paul's first journey. His mother, Eunice, and his grandmother taught Timothy a lot about the Old Testament through his childhood. He was shy but Paul trained and worked with him at Corinth and later at Ephesus. He was in Ephesus when Paul wrote two letters to him to encourage and teach him.

In 1 Timothy Paul mainly warns him to keep clear

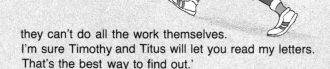

'An athlete who runs in a race cannot win the prize unless he obeys the rules.' (2 Tim 2:5)

of false teaching and fight against it with the truth, making sure that the right people are put in leadership positions (1 Tim 3:1–13).

In 2 Timothy Paul encourages him to go on well as a loyal soldier (2:3), not to be ashamed of Jesus (1:8), and to face up to those who are against the truth about Jesus. Timothy must go on preparing himself to do his job.

'Do your best to win full approval in God's sight, as a worker who is not ashamed of his work, one who correctly teaches the message of God's truth.' (2 Tim 2:15)

Titus went with Paul on some of his travels and was responsible for collecting famine relief funds for the Jerusalem church while he was at Corinth (See 2 Cor 8:6 and 16).

He was a good organiser and had more courage than Timothy. He helped the church at Corinth to accept Paul (see pages 112/113), and loved the Christians there; despite their problems he wanted to help them. Paul said, 'He is my partner and works with me to help you.' (2 Cor 8:23)

Titus worked with the church on the island of Crete. Paul wrote to him there about the sort of people who should be in leadership positions. One special need in Crete was for teaching on self-control! (2:2,5,6 and 12).

Paul reminded him that Jesus has saved us and we belong to him now.

'It was not because of any good deeds that we ourselves had done, but because of his own mercy that he saved us . . .' (Titus 3:5).

If people started stupid arguments Titus was not to waste time arguing (Titus 3:9–10).

THE TEAM TODAY

There it was! The 3.45 bell! 'Great,' thought Gavin, as he waited impatiently for 'Drone', their Maths teacher, to finish. 'Right, now into action', he said to himself. It was the meeting of the 'WATTS' group at 4.00 – it used to be 'Christian Union', but they renamed it Watts as in 'light'. So much to do, so little time – the room to be rearranged, video to set up, visiting speaker to be met at the entrance. Gavin had been thinking about this problem all day – which had earned him an extra essay on 'attentiveness'. The rest of the committee had got involved in other things, great in some ways because that sometimes meant that the Christians were in contact with other people but why on WATTS evenings? Dave was doing extra fitness training. Liz had made a coffee date, Vanessa 'had' to go home to watch TV, and Andy had made a feeble excuse about feeling a bit off-colour after the sausages at lunch.

'What can I do?' Gavin thought to himself.

He had left it a bit late really to do anything about it. Now he came to think about it, if he'd asked Mr Price to meet the speaker that would have left Gavin time to do the other things. He buzzed round getting hotter and hotter, room re-arranged, video set up ('strange, no-one here yet') – now down to the entrance.

And when Gavin and his guest arrived in the room there was still no-one there! And no-one did come to that meeting. Liz (publicity) had forgotten to hand out the invitation cards and get a notice into assembly. What a team! (see 2 Tim 2:3–7).

HEBREWS

KNOWING JESUS

HEBREWS

☐ **Written by** . . . Author unknown. A Greek-speaking Jew. Could be follower of Paul or collection of Paul's talks to Jewish Christians.

☐ **Written to** . . . A group of Jewish Christians who may have been thinking of turning back to their old beliefs. They found it hard to stand for Jesus against suffering.

Because they were Jews and knew the Old Testament well the writer is able to show them that all the Old Testament tells us about Jesus. We can find out a lot about Jesus by reading it, even in stories of Moses, or the prophets.

Here are some of the points in the letter to the Hebrews.

COVENANT

People in the Old Testament were used to legal agreements (covenants) binding nations together. The writer of Hebrews reminds them that God made a covenant between himself and the Jews which they constantly broke (see page 24.)

God made his covenant with Abraham and his sons, and reminded the people as they were to go into their new land –

'Has any god ever dared to go and take a people from another nation and make them his own as the Lord your God did for you in Egypt? . . . Because he loved your ancestors he chose you, and by his great power he himself brought you out of Egypt' (Deut 4:33–37).

God promised a new agreement (see Jeremiah 31:31–34). It was to be even better, because it was made possible by Jesus' sacrifice (see Heb 8 and 9).

'If there had been nothing wrong with the first covenant, there would have been no need for a second one. But God finds fault with his people when he says "The days are coming . . . when I will draw up a new covenant with the people . . . I will put my laws in their minds and write them on their hearts, I will be their God and they will be my people" ' (Heb 8:7,8,10).

In 672 BC, the King of Assyria made this covenant with the nations he ruled, showing the benefits of loyalty . . . and the penalties for rebellion!

TABERNACLE

While the Israelites travelled towards their new home the High Priest asked forgiveness and made sacrifices for them in the tabernacle – the 'tent-temple'. (See pages 23 and 25)

The writer says that Jesus is a High Priest who sacrificed in a 'perfect tent' – opening up heaven to those who trust him (Heb 9:1–25).

MOSES

Moses was great, but Jesus is even greater!

'Moses was faithful in God's house as a servant . . . But Christ is faithful as the Son in charge of God's house. We are his house . . .' (Heb 3:5–6).

PROPHETS (see pages 43, 56–65)

The prophets delivered God's message, but now someone even greater has come!

'. . . in these last days (God) has spoken to us through his Son.' (Heb 1:2)

No matter when people lived, or what problems they have, Jesus can be trusted!

'Remember your former leaders, who spoke God's message to you. Think back on how they lived and died and imitate their faith. Jesus Christ is the same yesterday, today and for ever' (Heb. 13:7–8).

JOSHUA AND AARON

Joshua led the people into the Promised Land (see pp 28/29), but he couldn't lead them to God's promised home – heaven! Only Jesus could do that (Heb 4:8–11).

Aaron and his descendants were High Priests with an unending job – bringing sacrifices to God, and giving God's forgiveness to the people. Jesus did this only once, but it was enough for everyone who follows him!

'The High Priest goes into the Most Holy Place every year with the blood of an animal. But Christ . . . was offered in sacrifice once to take away the sins of many' (Heb 9:25–28).

FAITH

All through the Old Testament there were people who trusted God; they had faith in him. Hebrews 11 is all about these people and the things God helped them to do.

Faith is 'to be sure of the things we hope for, to be certain of the things we cannot see' (Heb 11:1). We can be certain about these things because we can be certain about God!

Of course, we know about the great men of faith like Moses (though we often forget that they were ordinary like us, and had failings too), but what about Rahab, or Jephthah? They played their part in God's work too, as they trusted him, and found that he didn't let them down. You can read more about the people in this chapter; the Bible references are listed at the bottom of the page in the Good News Bible, or look them up in a Bible 'concordance', a book showing you where to find different words. (You could also try the index on page 134 of this book)

Getting to know a penfriend is a great adventure. Reading letters from him or her, exchanging photographs, perhaps talking with other people who know your friend. It's especially true of Jesus – the greatest friend there is!

He's given us so many different ways of learning about him that we couldn't possibly say, 'He didn't tell me about himself!'

The writer of this letter used the Old Testament and the lives of people through history to teach us something about following Jesus. You can use all of these and more!

As well as reading the Bible (which is the most important way) you can get booklets to help you understand what you read.

You could use Scripture Union's notes – 'One to One', or 'JAM' and others as you get older.

Books about other Christians can help; eg *The Hiding Place, Joni.*

You could ask people in your church, your minister or youth leader; and the more you find out about Jesus the more you can become like him.

KNOWING JESUS TODAY

All these can help us learn more about Jesus and how to follow him.

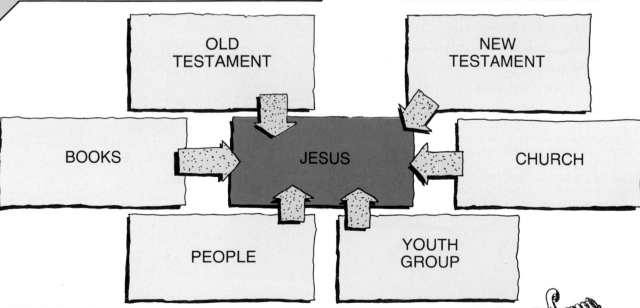

OLD TESTAMENT

NEW TESTAMENT

BOOKS

JESUS

CHURCH

PEOPLE

YOUTH GROUP

THE BIBLE

The whole Bible tells us the truth about Jesus and ourselves. It shows us our need to turn to Jesus.

'The word of God is alive and active, sharper than any double edged sword . . . there is nothing that can be hidden from God' (Heb. 4:12–13).

Like a good sword, the Bible cuts through the barriers we try to put up to hide what is really inside us.

JAMES
OBEYING JESUS

JAMES

☐ **Written by** . . . We're not certain, but probably James, Jesus' brother, the first leader of the church at Jerusalem. (Acts 12:17; Gal 1:19).

☐ **Written to** . . . Probably sent round to several churches of converted Jews, who needed help about how to live for Jesus.

While the writer to the Hebrews concentrated on *knowing* Jesus, James concentrated on *following* him in everyday life. The Christian needs both these letters!

BELIEVING AND DOING

Some of the Christians James wrote to seem to have misunderstood parts of what they had been taught, especially in some of Paul's letters. They thought, 'Belief and trust are all you need to be a Christian, you don't have to *do* any good things in life.' James showed that in *becoming* a Christian, believing and trusting are all we have to do, but *doing* what Jesus wants *shows* we are Christians!

'. . . what good is it for someone to say that he has faith if his actions do not prove it? . . . if faith is alone and includes no actions, then it is dead. Show me how anyone can have faith without actions. I will show you my faith by my actions' (James 2:14,17,18).

NO FAVOURITES

It's easy to let rich and nice-looking people have our time and attention, but Jesus gave his life for the poor and unlikeable people too.

'. . . you must never treat people in different ways according to their outward appearance . . . If you show more respect to the well-dressed man and say to him 'Have this best seat here', but say to the poor man 'Stand over there' . . . then you are guilty of making judgements based on evil motives' (James 2:1–4).

NOT THE WORLD'S WAY

The world tries to make us go its way, but James wanted his readers to submit to God instead. (See also Romans 12:2).

'Whoever wants to be the world's friend makes himself God's enemy . . . So then, submit to God, come near to God and he will come near to you' (James 4:4,7,8).

PATIENCE

If you have a garden you can't expect sudden results; but the flowers will grow!

Jesus seems a long time coming back, and evil seems to be staying around a long time. God's servants have always suffered with patience and God has shown them that he cared for them all along. In the meantime don't complain against each other!

'Be patient, then my brothers, until the Lord comes. See how patient a farmer is as he waits for his land to produce precious crops . . . You also must be patient . . . the day of the Lord's coming is near' (James 5:7,8).

Here are some of the things Jesus said which tie in with what James writes.

'. . . when you help a needy person, do it in such a way that even your closest friends will not know about it' (Matthew 6:3).

'. . . anyone who hears these words of mine and obeys them is like a wise man . . .' (Matthew 7:24). 'When you give a feast, invite the poor, the crippled, the lame, and the blind; and you will be blessed . . . God will repay you . . .' (Luke 14:13,14).

'. . . I was hungry and you fed me, thirsty and you gave me a drink . . . I was sick and you took care of me. Whenever you did this for one of the least important of these brothers of mine, you did it for me' (Matthew 25:35, 36, 40).

THE BIBLE

If God's word, the Bible, is a sword (see Hebrews) it must be used.

'Do not deceive yourselves by just listening to his word; instead put it into practice' (James 1:22).

Poverty, hunger and the results of wars are some of the ills in our world today which need Christian action.

THE TONGUE

James' readers had trouble controlling their tongues! They gossiped, criticized and tried to teach others before they were ready. The tongue is only a small part of us, but it causes a lot of trouble when it is misused. James reminded them how a bit can control a powerful horse, a small rudder can steer a great ship and a tiny spark can start a forest fire!

'. . . and the tongue is like a fire . . . It sets on fire the entire course of our existence . . . No one has ever been able to tame the tongue . . .' (Jas 3:6–8).

'Instead', says James, 'use the tongue for good, but you won't be able to if there is only evil inside.'

'. . . a grapevine cannot bear figs, nor can a salty spring produce fresh water' (Jas 3:12).

They're fitting more and more computers with voices. They are supposed to be 'user friendly' and should help the user relax and feel the computer cares about them!

I had a learning program which told me 'You have achieved the almost impossible by selecting all the wrong answers. How could you!!' But it really didn't care!

They can say things like 'Have a nice day' – but they don't care if you are run over by a bus. We can live in exactly the same way! James knew people who were just like that and he wanted them to put their Christianity into practice.

Instead of handing out words like 'I hope you're able to keep warm', or 'make sure you get enough to eat', people who are following Jesus need to take some action to back up their words, checking whether an old person has enough coal, taking a meal round to someone who lives on their own and is ill. Making our actions match our words.

1 AND 2 PETER, JUDE

PETER'S LIFE AND TEACHING

When the Emperor Nero (see p. 114) planned to kill the Christians, Peter wrote two letters to encourage them. He had learnt from the way Jesus had helped him through his mistakes. Both letters were sent round many churches, and the second was probably written shortly before his death, to help Christians to stand up against false teachers.

In his letters Peter looks back to some of the things that happened when he was with Jesus and the other disciples.

Peter was known as Simon when he was a fisherman with his brother Andrew. Jesus called him to follow him, and said he would 'catch men' instead of fish (Luke 5:9,10).

As one of Jesus' close friends Peter was with Jesus when he was transfigured at the top of the mountain (Mark 9:2–9).

Peter could say something very thoughtful and then spoil it by saying the first thing that came into his head. At Caesarea Philippi he said that Jesus was the Son of God and Jesus gave him his new name Peter, meaning 'a rock'. However, Peter then followed it by telling Jesus he was wrong about suffering and dying! (Matthew 16:13–23).

'He gave us new life by raising Jesus Christ from death. This fills us with a living hope, and so we look forward to possessing the rich blessings that God keeps for his people' (1 Peter 1:3–4).

'We have not depended on made-up stories in making known to you the mighty coming of our Lord Jesus Christ. With our own eyes we saw his greatness. We were there when he was given honour and glory by God the Father, when the voice came to him . . . (2 Peter 1:16–18).

'Come to the Lord, the living stone rejected by men as worthless but chosen by God as valuable. Come as living stones, and let yourselves be used in building the spiritual temple . . .' (1 Peter 2:4,5).

In an age when people valued fashion so much, Peter told them that God wants inner beauty more! (1 Peter 3:1–4).

Despite warnings, he ran away when Jesus was arrested. He even denied knowing Jesus. (Matthew 26:31–75).

'Have reverence for Christ in your hearts, and honour him as Lord. Be ready at all times to answer anyone who asks you to explain the hope you have in you . . . Happy are you if you are insulted because you are Christ's follower . . .' (1 Peter 3:15; 4:14).

Peter had failed Jesus, but Jesus had a private talk with him after he had been raised from the dead, to encourage him to be like a shepherd to Jesus' 'sheep'. (John 21:15–19).

'I, who am an elder myself, appeal to the church elders among you. I appeal to you to be shepherds of the flock that God gave you . . .' (1 Peter 5:1–2).

Peter went on to be the first preacher and leader of the church. (Acts 2:14–42) We think he was killed for Jesus in AD 64.

'. . . you must live the rest of your earthly lives controlled by God's will . . .' (1 Peter 4:2).

Peter knew that Jesus is the most important 'stone' in the building. Without him the rest fall apart.

Peter is known for his quick and ready response to situations, sometimes too quick! He was always ready to speak his mind, but without thinking through what he was saying. He was a leader but without the patience that leaders really need.

His tongue often got him into trouble, but despite his mistakes he was made one of the leaders of the disciples and then of the church as it grew.

Peter learnt from his mistakes. He looked back at the time he let Jesus down by denying that he knew Jesus and wrote to others, '. . . be ready at all times to answer anyone who asks you . . .'

We make mistakes but don't often *use* them. We usually:

- try to cover them up
- hope no-one noticed
- pretend we didn't make a mistake
- hope we'll forget them after a while

If Peter could have so many disasters and learn from them we can be encouraged to learn from our mishaps!

JUDE

☐ **Written by** . . . Jude the brother of Jesus and James. (see James)

☐ **Written to** . . . Unknown, but a group of Christians who, Jude knew, had trouble with false teachers.

There are such strong similarities between parts of Jude's letter and parts of Peter's second letter that it looks as if one copied from the other. Some think that Peter read Jude and wanted more people to read it so included it in his letter.

Though 'Jude' is very short – only one chapter – it helps us to see how empty some people are who spread false ideas about Jesus.

'They are like clouds carried along by the wind, but bringing no rain . . . like trees that bear no fruit . . .' v.12.

Though they are 'empty' they can cause division and Christians must be prepared . . .

'keep on building yourselves up.' v.20

The stories Jude includes in his letter seem strange to us. He used illustrations from the Old Testament and other Jewish books (the Apocrypha) – verses 9 and 14.

1, 2 AND 3 JOHN
UNDER ATTACK

AD 80   90   100

/DEATH OF
APOSTLE JOHN

John saw a great deal of persecution. The Emperor Nero killed many Christians in Rome and set off times of persecution in other areas. John's book *The Revelation* was written to help Christians going through very cruel times. However, even when Nero had gone, there were others who continued his cruelty. Usually people suspected of being Christians were put through a test. Would they offer incense at the shrine of the Emperor or another of the gods? If they did, they were free to go. True Christians would not worship at these shrines.

In about the year AD 112, the Roman Emperor Trajan sent his friend Pliny, an experienced lawyer, to sort out various problems in Bithynia (near the Black Sea). While he was there Christians were brought before him for judgement. These were the first he had met and he had to make his own rules. He wrote to Trajan reporting what he had decided to do . . .

'. . . If they admit they are Christians I ask them a second and third time, threatening capital punishment; if they persist I sentence them to death . . . There were others who displayed a like madness and whom I reserved to be sent to Rome, since they were Roman citizens . . . others who were accused worshipped your image and the statues of the gods, and cursed Christ . . . (Genuine Christians cannot be induced to curse Christ.) I feel I must consult you because it affects so many; for people of all ages and classes and of both sexes are being put into peril by accusation. This superstition has spread not only in the cities, but in the villages and rural districts as well; yet it seems capable of being checked . . . the temples which have almost been deserted, are beginning to be used again . . .'

Trajan replied . . .

'You have taken the right line, Pliny . . .'

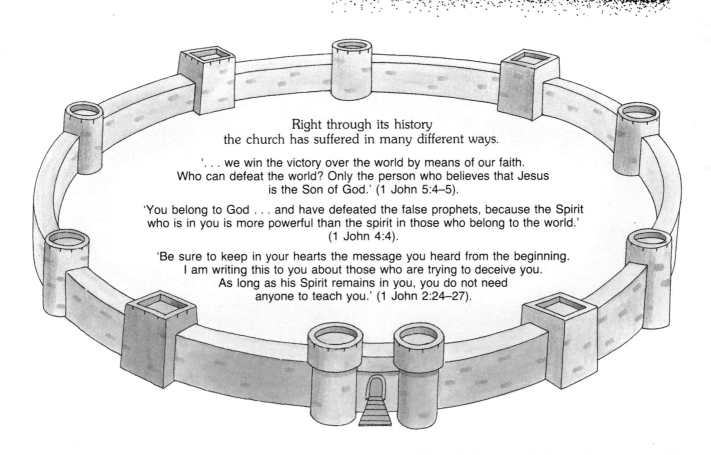

Right through its history
the church has suffered in many different ways.

'. . . we win the victory over the world by means of our faith.
Who can defeat the world? Only the person who believes that Jesus
is the Son of God.' (1 John 5:4–5).

'You belong to God . . . and have defeated the false prophets, because the Spirit
who is in you is more powerful than the spirit in those who belong to the world.'
(1 John 4:4).

'Be sure to keep in your hearts the message you heard from the beginning.
I am writing this to you about those who are trying to deceive you.
As long as his Spirit remains in you, you do not need
anyone to teach you.' (1 John 2:24–27).

It was up to the local 'police' to decide what to do in the towns. Sometimes they were good to the church, in other places they were cruel, doing more than the law allowed. Pleasing the mob was often more important than justice.

In AD 177 Christians in Lyons, France, sent a letter to friends about what had happened there . . .

'We cannot describe what has happened here, the extent of the rage of the (heathen) against God's people and the suffering of those who died. First they nobly endured the jostling rabble, they were hooted at, dragged about, stoned . . . and eventually brought to the forum to be examined before the mob . . . People falsely accused us of all kinds of things of which it is not lawful to speak or think, nor even to believe that any such things were ever done among men. Everyone was inflamed against us, so that even those who were moderate towards us through kinship were now greatly angered and raged against us . . . Pothinus our Bishop, more than 90 years old and quite feeble, was brought to the judgment seat and questioned. Those nearby hit him and kicked him, others threw whatever came to hand . . . so they thought to avenge their gods. . .'

Bettenson, *Documents of the Christian Church* (2nd ed. 1963). Oxford University Press.

Certificate of Sacrifice

To the Commissioners for Sacrifices in the village of Alexander's Island, from Aurelius Diogenes, son of Satabus, aged 72; scar on the right eyebrow.

I have always sacrificed to the gods, and now in your presence I have done sacrifice and poured libation and tasted the sacrifices, and I request you to certify to this effect.

Presented by me,

Aurelius Diogenes.

I certify that I witnessed his sacrifice,

Aurelius Syrus.

A libellus (certificate of sacrifice) discovered at Fayoum (Egypt) 1893; Milligan. Greek Papyri 48. 250A1.

A football team under attack by a powerful team may be able to win if they stay together. The last thing they want is team members going their own way! Unfortunately that's what happened in the church. Some of their teachers learnt ideas from other religions, Roman, Greek, Jewish and from the East, outside the Empire. They usually made up lies about Jesus and who he was. Some said that he wasn't God, some said he wasn't really a man. Ideas like these didn't just stay in their minds, they affected their family life and morals very badly. They were in danger of becoming just like the other religions.

False ideas were more dangerous to the church than persecution. Persecution makes Christians depend on each other more, false teaching divides them.

It has never been easy to be a Christian. If you are a Christian you have probably found it hard to tell others or stand up for what is right. And remember – it's not as bad in this country as in some others. The law and the authorities allow freedom of worship and witness – not all countries have this freedom. Even where the law allows freedom of worship, parents may not be able to teach their children or tell others about Jesus. Christians may be sent to psychiatric hospitals because they believe things that 'normal' people don't believe.

Try to imagine being in a Christian family where these things could happen. It could be frightening, but Christians have always proved that God gives the strength to overcome, and to love those who do these things to them!

'We love because God first loved us'. 1 John 4:19.

'Every child of God is able to defeat the world. And we win the victory over the world by means of our faith.' 1 John 5:4.

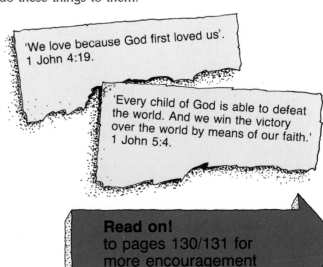

Read on! to pages 130/131 for more encouragement

JOHN

John, with his brother James, were ordinary fishermen in Galilee – nothing special ever really happened. Then Jesus called them to follow him. John probably didn't realize what that would mean. First, *he* had to change (they were hot tempered brothers – earning the nickname 'men of thunder', see Luke 9: 54 and Mark 3: 17). In fact, John became a special friend of Jesus, often at his side and very loyal. He was one of the three who went with Jesus to the top of a mountain and saw him with Moses and Elijah (Mark 9: 2–9). He was there at the cross; Jesus told John to look after Mary.

We don't know what happened to John later, he may have spent his later years at Ephesus; Polycarp knew him, and he was imprisoned at Patmos when he was old.

John wrote:
☐ **John's Gospel** – to tell people about Jesus (John 20: 30,31). See pages 87–89.
☐ **The three letters** – to help them to grow, 1 John 5: 13.
1 John . . . to Christians who had read his gospel
2 John . . . perhaps to an (unnamed) Christian lady; or was this a secret code for a church?
3 John . . . to Gaius, (a common name), who tried to help his fellow Christians despite opposition from Diotrephes, one of their own leaders!
☐ **The Revelation** – to encourage persecuted Christians

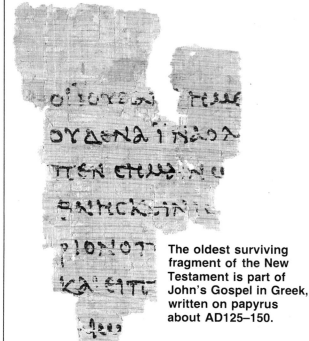

The oldest surviving fragment of the New Testament is part of John's Gospel in Greek, written on papyrus about AD125–150.

friends killed because they were Christians. The Roman Empire seemed like a monster in its harsh ways; but he knew that Jesus would defeat all evil, even the evils of Rome.

People are in prison today because they love and serve Jesus. Sometimes followers of Jesus are tempted to give up, though they may not be treated very harshly. But John's last book, the Revelation, shows that Jesus is fighting with them and he will win. He wants to share his victory with them! (see pages 132/133)

John was sure about Jesus! After all, he had been with him for over three years, and seen all that Jesus did. Though the whole world seemed to be fighting against the church, John knew they couldn't be separated from Jesus:

'We write to you about the Word of life . . . We have heard it, and we have seen it with our eyes; yes, we have seen it and our hands have touched it . . . What we have seen and heard we announce to you also . . .' 1 John 1:1–3.

When John wrote the Revelation he was an old man and a prisoner on the island of Patmos. He knew many were suffering or had seen relatives or close

Valeri Barinov, a Christian rock musician and evangelist, served a two and a half year sentence in a Soviet labour camp.

REVELATION
LETTERS TO SEVEN CHURCHES
CHAPTERS 1–3

It is not easy to understand The Revelation, but it's worth working at. The first three chapters are the easiest to grasp though they aren't so easy to put into practice! It's called 'the Revelation' because Jesus revealed his victory to John.

In a vision, John saw Jesus the King, in charge of the whole world and the church (the lamp-stands in Rev 1:20 and 2:1). He gave John letters to seven churches, groups of Christians who had many of the problems we have today.

☐ **Ephesus** (Rev 2:1–7) see pages 112, 116.
A church that was stuck in a rut, it wasn't really alive! (2:4). They served Jesus out of habit.

Who were the Nicolaitans? (v 6,15). We don't know exactly, they were probably named after their leader. They brought dangerous teaching into the church about who Jesus was and how people should live. Paul had warned the church leaders at Ephesus thirty years before that false teachers would come. (Ephesians 5:6; Acts 20:29, 30)

The theatre at Ephesus, holding 24,000 people, was built about 200BC

☐ **Smyrna** (Rev 2:8–11)
A suffering church – but loyal to Jesus.
Smyrna was famous for its arena and its games – perhaps many Christians died there. Though they were under the threat of death Jesus offered a 'victory crown' of new life! Winning athletes won a victory crown made of laurel leaves. The city is now called Izmir.

☐ **Pergamum** (Rev 2:12–17)
A church standing firm for Jesus despite the pressures around them. All cities had heathen temples but Pergamum was the headquarters of many of them. It was dominated by an altar to Zeus and was a centre for Caesar worship. There was one problem in the church – false ideas weakened them.

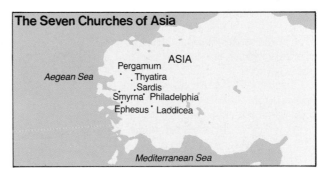

The Seven Churches of Asia

ASIA
Aegean Sea
Pergamum
Thyatira
Sardis
Smyrna Philadelphia
Ephesus Laodicea
Mediterranean Sea

☐ **Thyatira** (Rev 2:18–29)
'I know what you do, your love and faithfulness . . .' Great! – but they were allowing an evil woman to lead them, and to lead them into immorality.

☐ **Sardis** (Rev 3: 1–6)
People thought well of this church. It seemed to be going well but Jesus could see that there were problems. We don't know how it showed itself, but it seems that their lifestyle was affected, not just their thoughts.

☐ **Philadelphia** (Rev 3: 7–13)
A great church, following Jesus. Though they were a small group, and had to stand against opposition, they remained faithful to Jesus. Jesus promised to give them even more to do for him.

☐ **Laodicea** (Rev 3: 14–22)
A rich church. Like the town the church had plenty of money, but they were all show and did not really want to know or obey God well. Jesus offered to give a life that was worthwhile, something that no one could take away – as Jesus lived his life through them (see Luke 12, 13–21). 'Neither hot nor cold' 3: 16; – pipes brought hot spring water to the town, but it was lukewarm by the time it arrived.

REVELATION
GOD'S VICTORY
CHAPTERS 4–22

Do you know what these symbols are? The answers are at the bottom of the page.

It's useful to know what they mean.

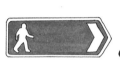

The book of Revelation uses many symbols. Some are fairly easy to understand.

Chapters 4–22 are about things which John couldn't describe with normal words. He tried to 'paint word-pictures.' In a vision Jesus showed him a little about the victory his people can share in.

DANGER
Some people try to work out what everything in the book means, even down to dates when it will happen. For example, someone has suggested that 'locusts' in chapter 9 means 'helicopters', with no particular reason. Some parts of the picture don't have any special meaning, and hunting for meanings can lead us away from the main point of the book. We can make it mean what *we* want, rather than listening to what God says. Arguments about these ideas have divided the church unnecessarily. They can stop us serving and loving Jesus.

GOD'S COMPLETE VICTORY
We use numbers to symbolize some things today. ('Number one' can mean 'the most important'.)

In Bible times the numbers four, seven and twelve meant 'perfect' or 'complete' even if the writer

didn't mean the literal numbers. For example ch. 21:16 – God's new city will be complete, it had four sides.

Don't try to follow the Revelation like a straight story. It's like a video shot from different angles but nearly all the tape out of the different cameras has been joined together so we see the same things several times over, (like soccer action replays from different angles). Then at the end there's the climax of the whole of history!

ANSWERS
Information Office
Camping
Pedestrian route
Roundabout

THE SEVEN CHURCHES Rev 1–3 A picture of the entire church. Some of the churches are praised for their obedience to God; others are warned of punishment. See page 131.

THE PAMPERED CITY CALLED BABYLON IS DESTROYED! Rev 17, 18 Babylon was the capital city of an evil empire which destroyed Jerusalem in 587BC. (see page 46) It is the symbol of evil in this world, – and Jesus is going to clear it away!

FINALLY

VICTO

Rev 19–22 And a great wedding feast, an unspoilt celebration of belonging to Jesus! And a new 'Jerusalem'–

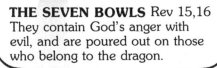

THE SEVEN BOWLS Rev 15,16 They contain God's anger with evil, and are poured out on those who belong to the dragon.

A GLIMPSE INTO HEAVEN ITSELF! Rev 4

Remember, it will be better than John's picture! Whatever it's like, it's a great place where we can really tell Jesus how much we love him.

WHAT A WAY TO END THE STORY OF THE BIBLE!

There has been a lot of struggling and sadness, and a lot of joy. God has been patient with his people despite their treatment of him. It is worthwhile after all – he is in charge and he will bring us through to victory!!!

THE SEVEN SEALS ON THE SCROLL Rev 5–7

Letters were rolled up and sealed with wax. This means the book about the future, which only Jesus can open. It included God's verdict on evil. (6; 12–17)

DO YOU WANT MORE TO READ AFTER THIS?

There's a book rather like the Revelation written by C. S. Lewis. It's called 'The Last Battle', the last part of the 'Narnia Chronicles'. Aslan the Lion (a symbol – as becomes clear) beats the forces of 'Tash', brings an end to the 'shadowlands' and begins the wonderful rule of the 'Narnia within Narnia' . . . but don't let me tell you, read it yourself!

RY!

God's city where all his people who trust in him will live for ever with him!

THE SEVEN TRUMPETS
Rev 8 to 11:19

Trumpets warned the defenders of a city or heralded the approach of the King! These trumpets warn us that God has judged the world and calls people to escape by turning back to him.

'. . . the dream is ended; this is morning.' And as He spoke He no longer looked to them like a lion; but the things that began to happen after that were so great and beautiful that I cannot write them . . . It was only the beginning of the real story. All their life in this world and all their adventures in Narnia had only been the cover and title page: now at last they were beginning Chapter One of the Great Story which no one on earth has read: which goes on for ever: in which every chapter is better than the one before.'

The Last Battle, C. S. Lewis

THE WOMAN, THE CHILD AND THE DRAGON Rev 12–14

The woman is a symbol of the church, the child is a symbol of Jesus; the dragon who tries to destroy them, is Satan, – though he is powerful he is defeated.

SOME BIBLE PEOPLE
AND WHERE TO FIND THEM

AARON Moses' brother. He helped Moses lead the Israelites and became the first High Priest. EXODUS 4,5,17,29,32

ABEL Second son of Adam and Eve. Murdered by his brother, Cain. GENESIS 4

ABRAHAM Founder of the Jewish nation. Abraham's wife was Sarah, and their son, Isaac. GENESIS 12,21,22

ADAM AND EVE The first man and woman. They disobeyed God and ate the forbidden fruit. GENESIS 1–3

ANDREW A fisherman. One of Jesus' twelve disciples and brother of Simon Peter. MATTHEW 4, JOHN 1 & 6

CORNELIUS A Roman centurion who was one of the first non-Jewish converts to Christianity. ACTS 11

DANIEL A prophet in exile in Babylon. He was loyal to God, who kept him safe in a den of lions. DANIEL 6

ELISHA He was Elijah's successor. He brought a boy back to life and healed Naaman of his leprosy. 2 KINGS 4,5

ESAU Sold his birthright to his twin brother, Jacob. GENESIS 25

ESTHER A Jewish girl who became queen of Persia and saved the Jewish nation from destruction. ESTHER

GOLIATH The Philistine giant killed by David. 1 SAMUEL 17

HEROD THE GREAT King of Judea when Jesus was born. Visited by the Wise Men. MATTHEW 2

ISAAC Son of Abraham and Sarah. Father of Jacob and Esau. GENESIS 21–26

JACOB Son of Isaac. Deceived Isaac into giving him the blessing meant for his brother, Esau. GENESIS 27

JAMES One of Jesus' closest disciples. He and his brother John were nicknamed 'Sons of Thunder'. MATTHEW 4,17

DAVID A shepherd boy who became a great soldier king of Israel. He was also a poet and wrote many Psalms. 1 SAMUEL 16–2 SAMUEL

ELIJAH A prophet sent by God to turn the Israelites from worshipping the idol, Baal. 1 KINGS 17, 18

EZEKIEL A Jewish prophet taken captive to Babylon. He foretold that one day the Jews would return and rebuild their city. EZEKIEL 1,36,37

GIDEON One of the judges of Israel. He led a small army of 300 men who defeated the Midianites. JUDGES 7,8

JOHN Brother of James. Known as the disciple whom Jesus loved. Wrote John's gospel, 1,2 and 3 John and Revelation. MATTHEW 10,17

JOHN THE BAPTIST Prepared the way for Jesus. Baptised many people. Was beheaded by Herod the Tetrarch. MATTHEW 3,14

JONAH A prophet whom God asked to go and preach to the people of Nineveh. He disobeyed God and was swallowed by a great fish. JONAH

JOSEPH (Old Testament) Favourite son of Jacob, sold into slavery in Egypt but later became prime minister. GENESIS 37,41

JOSEPH (New Testament) Husband of Mary, the mother of Jesus. A carpenter in Nazareth. MATTHEW 1, LUKE 2

JOSHUA After Moses died, he led the Israelites into the Promised Land. DEUTERONOMY 34, JOSHUA

LAZARUS Jesus brought him back to life. Jesus often visited Lazarus and his sisters, Mary and Martha. JOHN 11

MATTHEW A tax collector who became one of the twelve disciples and wrote a gospel. MATTHEW 9

MOSES The baby in the bullrushes who became the great leader of Israel. EXODUS 2–12

NOAH Built the Ark for his family and the animals to escape the Flood. GENESIS 7,8

PAUL First called Saul. A persecutor of Christians who was converted and became a great missionary traveller. Wrote thirteen New Testament books. ACTS 9–28

PETER A fisherman and one of Jesus' twelve disciples. He became a leader in the church. Wrote two New Testament letters. MATTHEW 16, 17, ACTS 1–15

PONTIUS PILATE Roman governor of Judea who ordered Jesus' crucifixion. MATTHEW 27

SAUL The first king of Israel. He turned against David and tried to kill him. 1 SAMUEL 10,18

SOLOMON King of Israel after David. Famous for his wisdom and riches. 1 KINGS 3

STEPHEN The first Christian martyr. ACTS 6,7

135

IMPORTANT PEOPLE AND EVENTS

OLD TESTAMENT

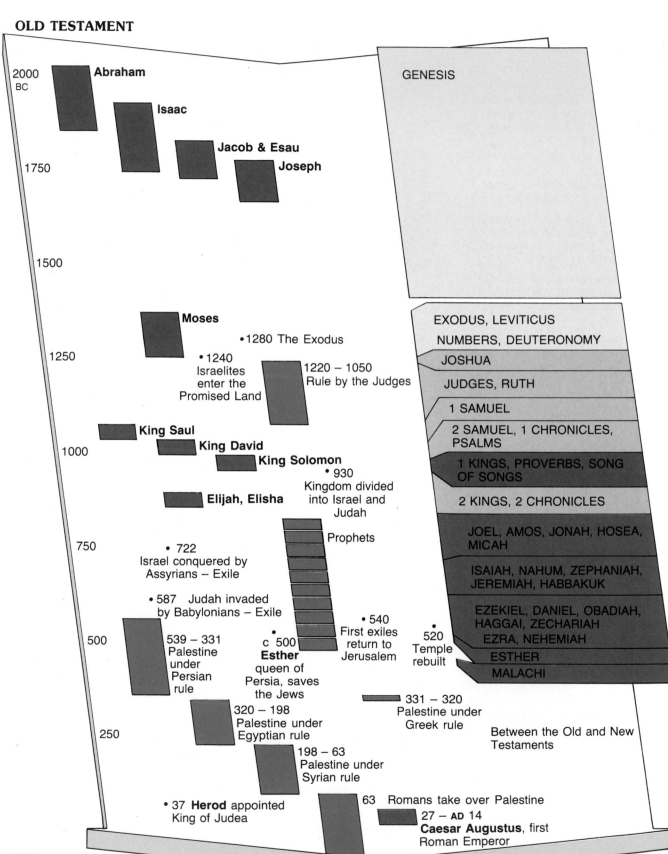

2000 BC

Abraham

Isaac

1750

Jacob & Esau

Joseph

GENESIS

1500

Moses

•1280 The Exodus

•1240 Israelites enter the Promised Land

1220 – 1050 Rule by the Judges

1250

EXODUS, LEVITICUS

NUMBERS, DEUTERONOMY

JOSHUA

JUDGES, RUTH

1 SAMUEL

King Saul

King David

1000

King Solomon

•930 Kingdom divided into Israel and Judah

Elijah, Elisha

2 SAMUEL, 1 CHRONICLES, PSALMS

1 KINGS, PROVERBS, SONG OF SONGS

2 KINGS, 2 CHRONICLES

Prophets

750

•722 Israel conquered by Assyrians – Exile

JOEL, AMOS, JONAH, HOSEA, MICAH

ISAIAH, NAHUM, ZEPHANIAH, JEREMIAH, HABBAKUK

•587 Judah invaded by Babylonians – Exile

•540 First exiles return to Jerusalem

•520 Temple rebuilt

EZEKIEL, DANIEL, OBADIAH, HAGGAI, ZECHARIAH

EZRA, NEHEMIAH

539 – 331 Palestine under Persian rule

c 500 **Esther** queen of Persia, saves the Jews

ESTHER

MALACHI

500

331 – 320 Palestine under Greek rule

320 – 198 Palestine under Egyptian rule

Between the Old and New Testaments

250

198 – 63 Palestine under Syrian rule

•37 **Herod** appointed King of Judea

63 Romans take over Palestine

27 – AD 14 **Caesar Augustus**, first Roman Emperor

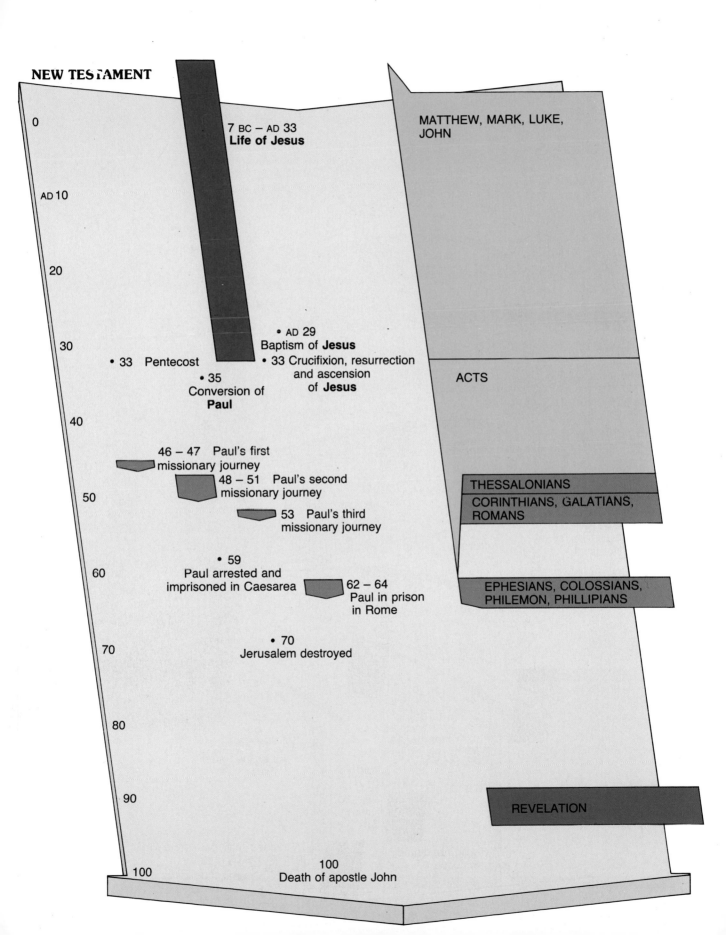

NEW TESTAMENT

0

AD 10

20

30

40

50

60

70

80

90

100

7 BC – AD 33
Life of Jesus

• AD 29
Baptism of **Jesus**

• 33   Pentecost

• 33 Crucifixion, resurrection
and ascension
of **Jesus**

• 35
Conversion of
Paul

46 – 47   Paul's first
missionary journey

48 – 51   Paul's second
missionary journey

53   Paul's third
missionary journey

• 59
Paul arrested and
imprisoned in Caesarea

62 – 64
Paul in prison
in Rome

• 70
Jerusalem destroyed

100
Death of apostle John

MATTHEW, MARK, LUKE,
JOHN

ACTS

THESSALONIANS

CORINTHIANS, GALATIANS,
ROMANS

EPHESIANS, COLOSSIANS,
PHILEMON, PHILLIPIANS

REVELATION

THE LANDS OF THE BIBLE

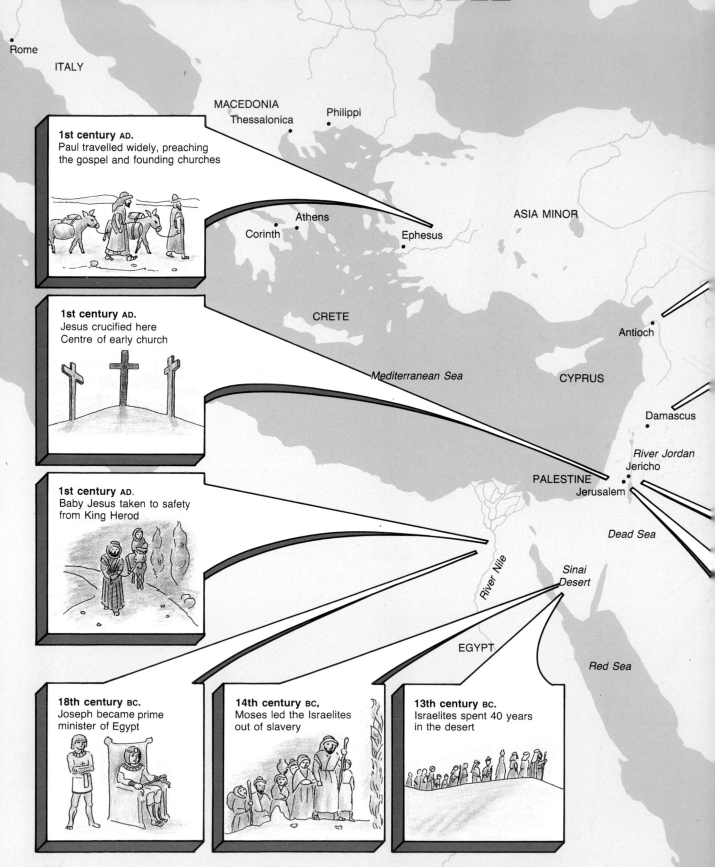

Rome

ITALY

MACEDONIA

Thessalonica

Philippi

1st century AD.
Paul travelled widely, preaching
the gospel and founding churches

ASIA MINOR

Athens

Corinth

Ephesus

CRETE

1st century AD.
Jesus crucified here
Centre of early church

Antioch

Mediterranean Sea

CYPRUS

Damascus

River Jordan

Jericho

PALESTINE

Jerusalem

1st century AD.
Baby Jesus taken to safety
from King Herod

Dead Sea

River Nile

Sinai
Desert

EGYPT

Red Sea

18th century BC.
Joseph became prime
minister of Egypt

14th century BC.
Moses led the Israelites
out of slavery

13th century BC.
Israelites spent 40 years
in the desert

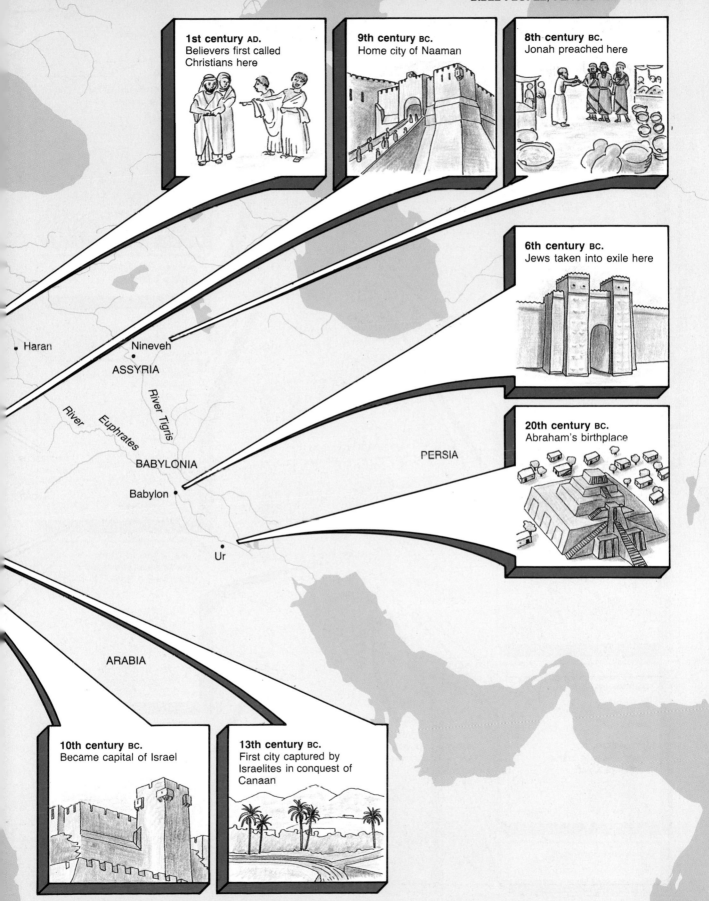

1st century AD.
Believers first called
Christians here

9th century BC.
Home city of Naaman

8th century BC.
Jonah preached here

6th century BC.
Jews taken into exile here

20th century BC.
Abraham's birthplace

Haran

Nineveh

ASSYRIA

River Tigris

River Euphrates

BABYLONIA

Babylon

Ur

PERSIA

ARABIA

10th century BC.
Became capital of Israel

13th century BC.
First city captured by
Israelites in conquest of
Canaan

PALESTINE AT THE TIME OF JESUS

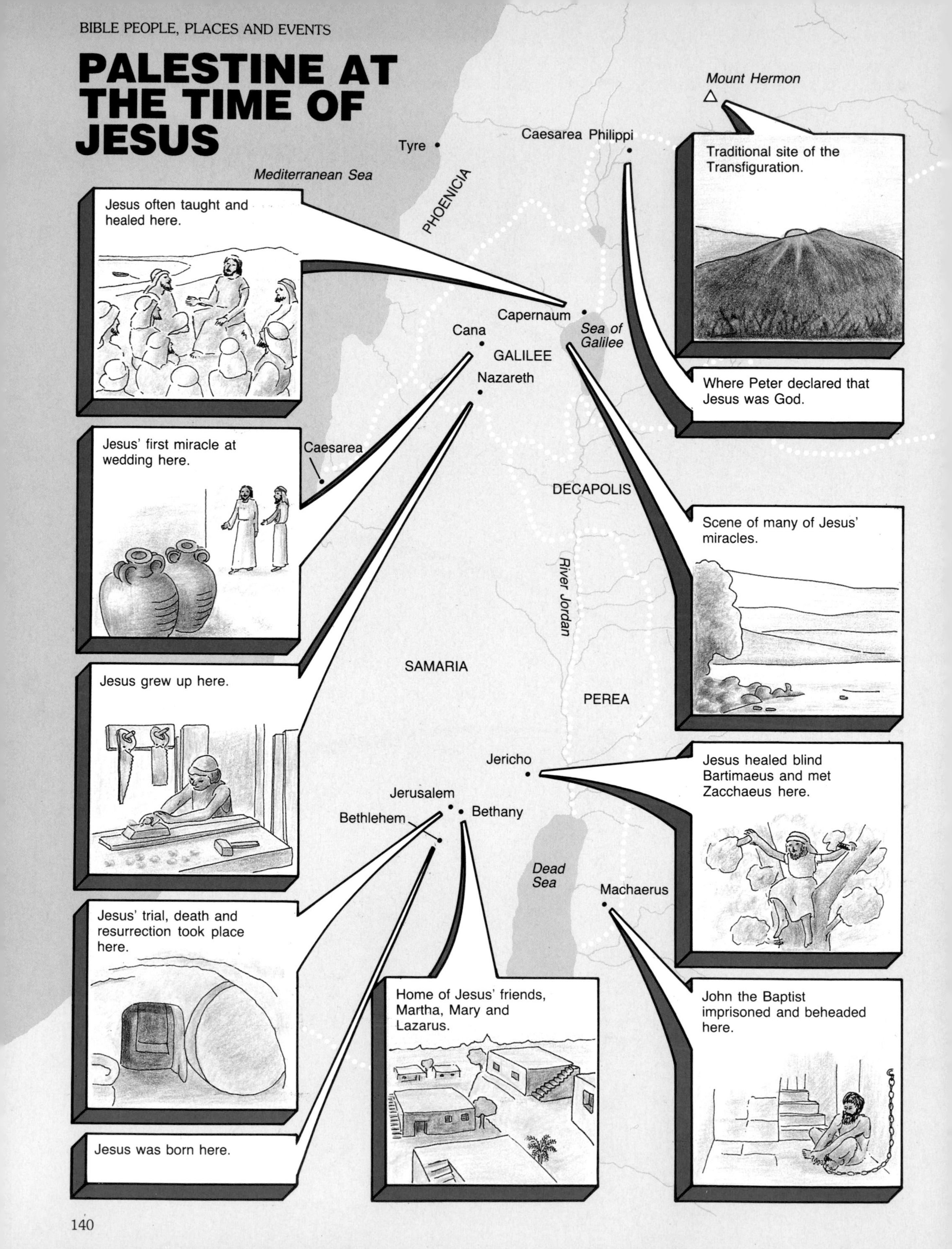

Mount Hermon

Tyre •

Mediterranean Sea

Caesarea Philippi •

PHOENICIA

Jesus often taught and healed here.

Traditional site of the Transfiguration.

Capernaum

Cana •

Sea of Galilee

GALILEE

Nazareth

Where Peter declared that Jesus was God.

Jesus' first miracle at wedding here.

Caesarea •

DECAPOLIS

River Jordan

Scene of many of Jesus' miracles.

SAMARIA

PEREA

Jesus grew up here.

Jericho •

Jesus healed blind Bartimaeus and met Zacchaeus here.

Jerusalem

Bethlehem

• Bethany

Dead Sea

• Machaerus

Jesus' trial, death and resurrection took place here.

Home of Jesus' friends, Martha, Mary and Lazarus.

John the Baptist imprisoned and beheaded here.

Jesus was born here.

JERUSALEM – THE HOLY CITY

Two views of Jerusalem – the city today and as it was in New Testament times.

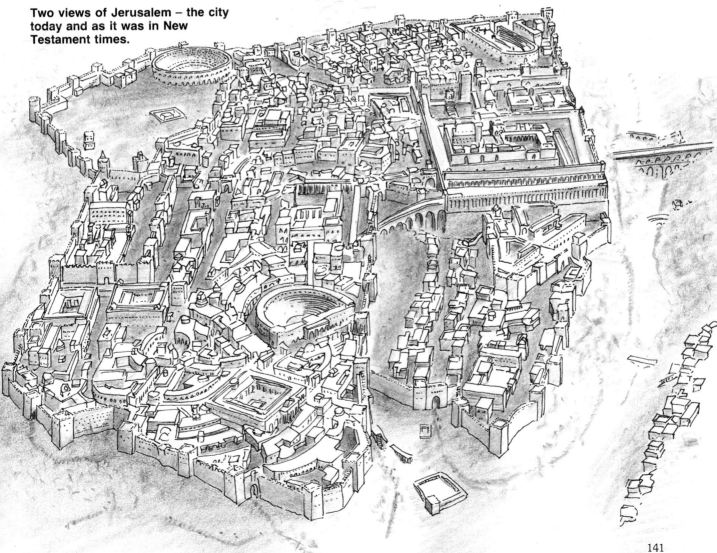

INDEX